RAND NATIONAL SECURITY RESEARCH DIVISION

SMART Security Cooperation Objectives

Improving DoD Planning and Guidance

Michael J. McNerney, Jefferson P. Marquis, S. Rebecca Zimmerman, Ariel Klein

Prepared for the Office of the Secretary of Defense

Approved for public release; distribution unlimited

For more information on this publication, visit www.rand.org/t/RR1430

Library of Congress Cataloging-in-Publication Data is available for this publication.
ISBN: 978-0-8330-9430-8

Published by the RAND Corporation, Santa Monica, Calif.

Preface

The U.S. Department of Defense (DoD) cooperates with U.S. interagency and foreign counterpart organizations around the world to achieve common security goals. Translating those goals into effective action requires deliberate, sophisticated planning based on well-designed objectives. Such planning is challenging, however, given the multitude of stakeholders, changing political and security environments, and resource limitations. Despite steady progress in recent years, DoD continues to face challenges developing security cooperation objectives that are specific, measurable, achievable, relevant and results-oriented, and time-bound ("SMART"). The acronym SMART has been used for several decades in the private sector, and it captures quite well the attributes that effective objectives appear to share. Recognizing this, DoD's 2010 Security Cooperation Reform Task Force highlighted the need to develop SMART objectives to ensure that limited security cooperation resources were properly directed for greatest effect. Equally important to designing SMART objectives is the ability to integrate them into a system for assessing, monitoring, and evaluating security cooperation programs and activities. This report evaluates DoD's effectiveness in developing SMART security cooperation objectives that facilitate assessment, monitoring, and evaluation. It also proposes a systematic approach to developing security cooperation objectives for use by policymakers, planners, program managers, and resource managers.

This report should be valuable for defense and foreign policy analysts with an interest in security cooperation.

This research was sponsored by the Deputy Assistant Secretary of Defense for Security Cooperation and conducted within the International Security and Defense Policy Center of the RAND National Defense Research Institute, a federally funded research and development center sponsored by the Office of the Secretary of Defense, the Joint Staff, the Unified Combatant Commands, the Navy, the Marine Corps, the defense agencies, and the defense Intelligence Community.

For more information on the RAND International Security and Defense Policy Center, see www.rand.org/nsrd/ndri/centers/isdp or contact the director (contact information is provided on the web page).

Contents

Figures and Tables

Figures

Tables

Summary

The U.S. Department of Defense (DoD) cooperates with U.S. interagency and foreign counterparts around the world in pursuit of common security interests. Those interests are fairly easy to understand at a broad level: regional stability, counterterrorism, military professionalism, etc. Translating these interests into effective action, however, is a complicated endeavor requiring rigorous planning. Since the mid-1990s, security cooperation has become increasingly well embedded in strategic DoD planning. Objectives of various types (end states, goals, etc.) exist at many planning levels, including policy, regional, country, and activity. While aligning and rationalizing these objectives within various plans has improved, making them detailed enough so that leaders can understand the extent to which security cooperation efforts are succeeding or failing remains particularly challenging.

The 2010 Security Cooperation Reform Task Force identified poorly defined country objectives as a significant weak link in prioritizing resource allocation. It highlighted a need for DoD to develop country strategies and associated "SMART" (specific, measurable, achievable, relevant and results-oriented, and time-bound) objectives to ensure that limited security cooperation resources were properly directed for greatest effect. The Defense Institute of Security Assistance Management also references the need for SMART objectives in its August 2015 textbook, *The Management of Security Cooperation*.[1]

[1] Defense Institute of Security Assistance Management, *The Management of Security Cooperation* ("Green Book"), August 2015, p. 19-4.

Security cooperation objectives are the foundation of a system that allows policymakers and planners to assess foreign defense partners, monitor the performance of security cooperation programs, and evaluate their effectiveness. Rigorous assessment, monitoring, and evaluation (AME) requires clarity of purpose and a detailed roadmap, despite imperfect information, dynamic political and security environments, uncertain long-term resources, and diverse stakeholders—most importantly, the foreign partners themselves. SMART objectives, like defense planning in general, are important because they drive challenging, iterative dialogues among decisionmakers who must link strategies to tasks.

Office of the Secretary of Defense (OSD) officials and DoD's combatant command (CCMD) planners recognize these challenges and have taken some initial steps to improve both security cooperation objectives and the plans and systems in which they are embedded. Through written guidance, training, and countless informal discussions, OSD officials have discussed the concept of SMART objectives. CCMD planners have incorporated the idea to varying degrees in the way they develop objectives in their various plans. For example, some CCMD staff talk explicitly about SMART objectives at conferences and with U.S. embassy colleagues. Despite this, it remains difficult for OSD senior leaders to understand how effectively DoD as a whole is setting clear, actionable objectives and then conducting AME to understand DoD's progress toward those objectives. And it remains challenging for CCMD leaders to ensure that the hundreds of stakeholders involved in security cooperation planning and implementation are systematically learning and applying the concept of SMART objectives and using it to facilitate effective AME. We hope that findings and recommendations in this report will help partner-nation officials, U.S. planners and program implementers, and OSD, Joint Staff, State Department, and congressional overseers better understand their common objectives, which should help them to support efforts that are working and redirect or abandon those that are not.

Study Goals and Tasks

This study had two principal goals: (1) help determine DoD effectiveness in establishing and prioritizing security cooperation objectives and assessing, monitoring, and evaluating security cooperation programs and activities and (2) propose and test a systematic approach to security cooperation objective development that could be readily and usefully adopted by CCMDs and incorporated into DoD-wide guidance.

To help achieve these goals, we undertook the following research tasks:

1. We analyzed existing strategic-, operational-, and country-level security cooperation planning and AME practices and connections. This involved conducting interviews with senior leaders, strategists, planners, programmers, assessors, and practitioners in OSD, the CCMDs, U.S. embassy–based security cooperation organizations (SCOs), and other government agencies to determine the extent to which they find security cooperation objectives appropriately specified, aligned, prioritized, and measured. We also discussed how stakeholders interpret security cooperation guidance, particularly whether it was sufficiently clear, detailed, and flexible.
2. We adapted and expanded SMART objective-setting criteria that have been long employed by strategic planners in the business world and have been more recently used by DoD planners to varying degrees. We then evaluated country security cooperation objectives associated with 18 partner nations in four geographic CCMDs: U.S. European Command (EUCOM), U.S. Pacific Command (PACOM), U.S. Southern Command (SOUTHCOM), and U.S. Central Command (CENTCOM), based on a set of binary questions that we developed to clarify each SMART criterion. In the cases of EUCOM, PACOM, and SOUTHCOM, we presented our evaluation of existing security cooperation objectives, along with illustrative alternative objectives, to CCMD country desk officers responsible for the selected partners. These experts provided feedback on

our analysis, as well as their perspectives on country objective development.

3. Based on the research findings resulting from the previous two tasks, we recommended changes to security cooperation guidance and planning that would enable
   - OSD to better communicate its intent to CCMD security cooperation planners, program managers, and resource providers
   - CCMDs to improve their processes for developing country plan objectives using SMART criteria
   - security cooperation staff to retain the skills necessary to develop and utilize SMART objectives.

Planning and AME Findings

As we discuss in Chapters Three, Four, and Five, the CCMDs have taken important steps toward improving security cooperation planning. As illustrated by the experiences of PACOM, EUCOM, and SOUTHCOM, however, there is still room for improvement in the areas of developing SMART objectives and conducting AME.

U.S. Pacific Command

While recognizing the need for continued improvements, PACOM officials have made improvements to the way they conduct security cooperation planning and AME. In particular, they focused on making the 2015 version of PACOM's overarching plan for the Asia-Pacific region—the Theater Campaign Plan (TCP)—easier to understand and utilize for AME, including by reducing the number of TCP intermediate military objectives (IMOs). PACOM has a well-developed framework for evaluating IMOs associated with its major lines of effort, which now include allies and prioritized emerging partners. Furthermore, PACOM's process of bringing together all the key security cooperation stakeholders in biannual working groups focused on partner capability development is a best practice worth highlighting.

In spite of these improvements and robust coordination processes, the connections among theater campaign planning, security cooperation country planning, and AME are not as tight as they could be. One reason for this is the lack of well-accepted country objectives to guide security cooperation planning and help ensure the alignment of security cooperation ends, ways, and means. Another recognized shortcoming is PACOM's AME process for security cooperation. Despite the effort to simplify its TCP, the way that PACOM conducts AME is complex and does not extend to the country level. Fortunately, PACOM's emphasis on creating capability development roadmaps for partner nations may provide the foundation on which to build an improved AME process.

U.S. European Command

EUCOM's processes for security cooperation objective-setting and AME are the work of many years of systematic development. EUCOM has developed customized tools for prioritizing the many objectives in this complex area of operations, as well as a customized system for tracking progress toward objectives, called SAS Plan.[2] Objective-setting at EUCOM primarily serves to harmonize guidance and is largely top-down. Efforts at AME are captured in SAS Plan in the form of self-assessments that feed into higher-level assessments done by J7 (Exercises and Assessment) assessment staff. As discussed in the full report, we assessed that the process overall is robust and that all parties appear to understand it.

However, EUCOM faces several challenges to security cooperation. First, security cooperation objectives are coordinated among three parties: the office of primary responsibility (OPR), the SCO/senior defense official (SDO), and the EUCOM country desk officer. While revisions to the process may change this soon, at the time of writing there was no occasion where those three parties conversed as a group. Second, OPR officials, who have primary responsibility for authorship, may not have familiarity with the countries whose objectives they are

---

[2] *SAS Plan* stands for Strategy for Active Security Plan; however, that term is no longer in use.

writing and, depending on the office, may have large numbers of objectives to write. Third, SCO/SDOs working in the partner nation find it harder to access the SAS Plan system, making it difficult for them to take an active part in discussions. (This too may be under revision and access may be expanded.) Finally, in the area of AME, processes are nearly all based on self-assessment or the counting of very basic event-level data. The system, while rigorous in its design, lacks a way to consistently test security cooperation hypotheses or analyze outcomes.

U.S. Southern Command

SOUTHCOM has a well-structured and comprehensive process for developing its TCP and country cooperation plans (CCPs). For example, its Phase Zero Nesting Model helps demonstrate linkages between country-level activities and strategic-level guidance. SOUTHCOM has worked to develop both SMART objectives and a SMART security cooperation planning system. By designating responsible stakeholders, measurable indicators, and manageable timelines, among other concerns raised in the RAND framework, the system provides a practical means of translating SOUTHCOM's theater end states into operational activities. Given the 2015 change in the nesting model to remove specified tasks, milestones, and targeted capabilities from SOUTHCOM's TCP, there is a risk that details important to ensuring "SMARTness" at the CCMD level will be lost. If security cooperation planners manage the linkages between SCOs and CCMD staff well, however, this risk should be mitigated, and SOUTHCOM's architecture for nesting hierarchical objectives could potentially inform the approaches of other CCMDs.

Despite its robust objective development process, SOUTHCOM lacks a rigorous and in-depth AME framework. Due mainly to reductions in AME personnel, planners have devised individualized ad hoc systems that are not easily integrated for review at higher levels, which thus impedes analysis-based decisionmaking. Still, the otherwise robust planning process should allow for a migration to a more rigorous AME framework, and SOUTHCOM officials are making progress toward a more comprehensive and effective evaluation system.

Objective Evaluation Findings

In Chapters Three, Four, and Five, we discuss our findings from our SMART evaluation of selected country objectives in PACOM, EUCOM, and SOUTHCOM. Here, we summarize those findings by looking at the general trends across these CCMDs.

Although the SMARTness of existing security cooperation objectives varied considerably, we observed some general trends in the extent to which CCMD country objectives were in line with SMART criteria. As Table S.1 indicates, individual objectives proved unsatisfactory according to the majority of our evaluation criteria. Although generally relevant and results-oriented, they were neither specific nor measurable nor time-bound. We could not determine whether they were achievable through documentary evidence.

General Findings and Recommendations

By most accounts, OSD, CCMDs, the Joint Staff, and other organizations supporting security cooperation efforts benefit from more robust planning and coordination overall than ever before. Guidance has become more detailed regarding goals and expectations. Planning is robust and involves many stakeholders. Coordination is facilitated through formal and informal communication, as well as workshops focusing on various segments of the security cooperation community.

Nevertheless, DoD does not yet have a sufficiently standardized and integrated approach to security cooperation planning—particularly in the areas of objective development and AME that would enable DoD leaders, the administration, and Congress to gauge the extent to which global security cooperation resources are being appropriately targeted and effectively employed. Furthermore, the lack of SMART objectives, particularly at the country level, is an important reason why it has been difficult to establish a firm connection between the partnering goals expressed in national strategy documents and the actual activities being conducted by, with, and through partner nations.

Table S.1
Summary of SMART Evaluation

Criterion	Summary of Evaluation	Summary of Weaknesses
Specific	Mixed results, but most objectives not satisfactory	• Multiple outcomes conflated within one objective • Unclear what needed to be done • Unclear responsibilities
Measurable	Most objectives unsatisfactory—poorest of criteria we were able to evaluate	• Unclear baseline • Unclear units of measure • Insufficient intermediate measures
Achievable	Unable to evaluate	• Assessments of partner and operating environment not documented • To the extent relevant analysis existed, it was not well incorporated into the development of security cooperation objectives
Relevant and results-oriented	Most objectives satisfactory and aligned with higher-level guidance	
Time-bound	Most objectives unsatisfactory	• Few concrete time horizons • Unclear relationship between time to achieve and resources available

Table S.2 presents general findings from our analyses of CCMD planning, AME, and country objectives, along with associated recommendations intended to help improve OSD, Joint Staff, and CCMD guidance, plans, and processes related to security cooperation. These findings and recommendations are discussed in detail in Chapter Six.

Table S.2
Analyses of CCMD Planning and AME Country Objectives

General Finding	Recommendation
1. Most individual country objectives were not SMART.	1. OSD should provide SMART criteria and prioritization guidance to CCMDs and evaluate their performance accordingly.
2. CCMD security cooperation planning was SMARTer than individual country objectives.	2. OSD and the Joint Staff should work with CCMDs to create a SMART security cooperation planning system centered on country plans. Creating SMART country objectives is not enough.
3. CCMD security cooperation planning could benefit from greater standardization.	3. OSD and the Joint Staff should work with CCMDs to establish a common theater planning hierarchy for security cooperation objectives, with standard terminology and a standard SMART-objective review process.
4. Responsibility and priority for developing country objectives differed by CCMD.	4. CCMDs should integrate security cooperation elements of planning under a single authority.
5. Understanding of the SMART concept varied among stakeholders.	5. DoD should incorporate the SMART concept more formally into security cooperation training.
6. SMART objectives did not adequately serve as a foundation for security cooperation AME.	6. OSD should establish a security cooperation framework that links SMART objectives to AME processes and requirements at the strategic and country levels.

Acknowledgments

We deeply appreciate the assistance provided by our sponsor, Deputy Assistant Secretary of Defense for Security Cooperation Tommy Ross; his director for Partnership Policy and Strategy, Ron Meyers; and Ron's predecessor, Alan Gorowitz. We are also grateful to their colleagues, who provided important insights throughout our research.

We also recognize the invaluable contributions of those experts we interviewed at several DoD combatant commands and U.S. embassies. These include officials in PACOM's J45 (Security Assistance and Cooperative Program Division), J5 (Strategic Planning and Policy Directorate), J8 (Resources and Assessments Directorate), and J9 (Pacific Outreach Directorate); EUCOM's J5/J8 (Policy, Strategy, Partnering and Capabilities Directorate) and J7 (Exercises and Assessments Directorate); SOUTHCOM's J5 (Strategy, Policy, and Plans Directorate), J8 (Resources and Assessments Directorate), and J9 (Partnering Directorate); and security cooperation officers at several embassies.

We also thank our reviewers, Jennifer Moroney and James Schear, whose comments improved the report tremendously.

Finally, we recognize the administrative support provided by Betsy Kammer and Theresa DiMaggio and the professional editing provided by James Torr.

CHAPTER ONE

Introduction

Effective planning can help the United States overcome challenges and seize opportunities to strengthen its security sector partnerships around the world. Since the mid-1990s, the U.S. Department of Defense (DoD) has made steady progress in integrating security cooperation into national and regional strategies and plans, understanding the scope of security cooperation activities across the globe, and facilitating collaboration among the many security cooperation stakeholders within and outside the department. However, there is wide acknowledgment that the effectiveness of DoD security cooperation programs and activities is limited by a number of systemic weaknesses, including immature and detached country planning and inconsistent and subjective assessment, monitoring, and evaluation (AME) processes.[1]

An important factor underlying these weaknesses is a lack of specific, measurable, achievable, relevant and results-oriented, and time-bound ("SMART") country objectives in standardized, regularly published planning documents. Nor is the progress toward the accomplishment of country objectives in terms of outcomes and impact (as opposed to inputs and outputs) evaluated using a common set of metrics and relevant qualitative and quantitative data analyzed by unbiased AME and subject-matter experts. As a result, it is often unclear

[1] For a fuller discussion of DoD security cooperation system weaknesses, see U.S. Department of Defense Security Cooperation Reform Task Force, *Phase I Report*, 2011. See also Defense Institute of Security Assistance Management, *The Management of Security Cooperation* ("Green Book"), August 2015, Appendix 2: History of Security Assistance and Security Cooperation.

how well security cooperation activities align with U.S. national security priorities. Not only does this make it difficult for DoD to justify continued security cooperation funding in a fiscally constrained environment, it also hampers the department's ability to shape the global security landscape in a way that both reduces the risk of large-scale U.S. military involvement in conflicts and prepares U.S. and allied forces for future threats.

What Are SMART Objectives?

In any enterprise, there are tasks that must be managed in order for the organization to succeed. In large organizations with complex missions, deciding which tasks to do and determining the extent to which the organization has succeeded in accomplishing them can be difficult. Most organizations, consciously or not, engage in some kind of goal- or objective-setting behavior in order to identify and execute the right activities to succeed. Choose the right goals and the enterprise is spurred toward success; choose the wrong goals and it stalls or veers off course. There are numerous processes that can be used to craft good objectives, but there are certain attributes that well-written objectives appear to share. A common way to describe those attributes is using the mnemonic device SMART. As Table 1.1 shows, one of the conceptual shortcomings with this device is that there is no consensus on the exact terminology attached to the letters in SMART.[2] Despite this lack of clarity—some constructs even add letters to make the acronym SMARTER—there is a clear mainstream of thought as to the SMART concept more generally.

For the purposes of analyzing DoD security cooperation efforts, we chose to interpret the SMART criteria using the most common terminology we found: specific, measurable, achievable, relevant and results-oriented, and time-bound.

---

[2] George T. Doran, "There's a S.M.A.R.T. Way to Write Management's Goals and Objectives," *Management Review*, Vol. 70, No. 11, 1981, p. 35.

Table 1.1
Terms Associated with the Mnemonic SMART

Letter	Common Terms
S	Specific, significant, stretching, simple, stimulating, succinct, straightforward, self-owned, self-managed, self-controlled, strategic, sensible
M	Measurable, meaningful, motivational, manageable, magical, magnetic, maintainable, mapped to goals
A	Agreed upon, attainable, achievable, acceptable, action-oriented, attributable, actionable, appropriate, ambitious, aspirational, accepted/acceptable, aligned, accountable, agreed, adapted, as-if-now
R	Realistic, relevant, reasonable, rewarding, results-oriented, resources are adequate, resourced, recorded, reviewable, robust, relevant to a mission
T	Time-based, timely, tangible, trackable, tactical, traceable, toward what you want, and many starting with "time-" (e.g., -limited, -constrained)
E/R	Ethical, exciting, enjoyable, extending, evaluated, engaging, energizing Recorded, reviewed, rewarded, realistic, relevant, resourced, research-based

SOURCE: D. T. Wade, "Goal Setting in Rehabilitation: An Overview of What, Why and How," *Clinical Rehabilitation*, Vol. 23, No. 4, April 1, 2009, p. 294.

Study Goals and Focus

This study had two principal goals: (1) help analyze DoD effectiveness in establishing and prioritizing security cooperation country objectives and assessing, monitoring, and evaluating security cooperation programs and activities and (2) propose and test a systematic approach to security cooperation objective development that could be readily and usefully adopted by combatant commands (CCMDs) and incorporated into DoD-wide guidance.

To accomplish these goals, we focused our research efforts on three related components of the overall security cooperation planning and execution process: (1) Office of the Secretary of Defense (OSD) planning guidance to the CCMDs, (2) security cooperation–associated lines of effort or activity included in the CCMDs' Theater Campaign Plans (TCPs), and (3) CCMD country security cooperation plans (CSCPs) for selected U.S. partner nations. In addition, we conducted a preliminary investigation of the AME practices carried out by the

CCMDs to improve their security cooperation planning and execution, and we report on their progress in achieving their country and regional objectives. Another RAND study will build on these initial results in order to present OSD with alternative frameworks for assessing, monitoring, and evaluating the results of security cooperation programs across the department.

The DoD security cooperation community does not yet employ a common departmental lexicon similar to what is used by the State Department and the U.S. Agency of International Development, among others. With the exception of some AME experts we interviewed, most security cooperation staff do not distinguish among assessment, monitoring, and evaluation, and they tend to describe all three functions as aspects of assessment. This report defines the three terms as follows:

- *Assessment* is an analysis of preexisting environmental conditions (e.g., existing partner capabilities) that could affect or influence the success of an existing or planned security cooperation program or line of effort/activity.
- *Monitoring* is a continuous process designed to provide program and activity managers with regular feedback on the extent to which the near-term results related to an ongoing program or line of effort/activity are in accordance with expectations.
- *Evaluation* is the periodic collection and analysis of information and evidence regarding the extent to which security cooperation objectives related to security cooperation programs or lines of effort/activity have been achieved.

Figure 1.1 depicts our understanding of how these three security cooperation components fit within the overall process. Thus, our study focus areas provide direction to those responsible for executing security cooperation programs and activities, as do State Department and service guidance and plans. Furthermore, as the arrows indicate, OSD and CCMD planning documents are developed in coordination with State Department foreign assistance guidance and regional and country plans, and these documents influence and are influenced by the services' headquarters security cooperation guidance and component

Figure 1.1
Security Cooperation Planning and Execution Process

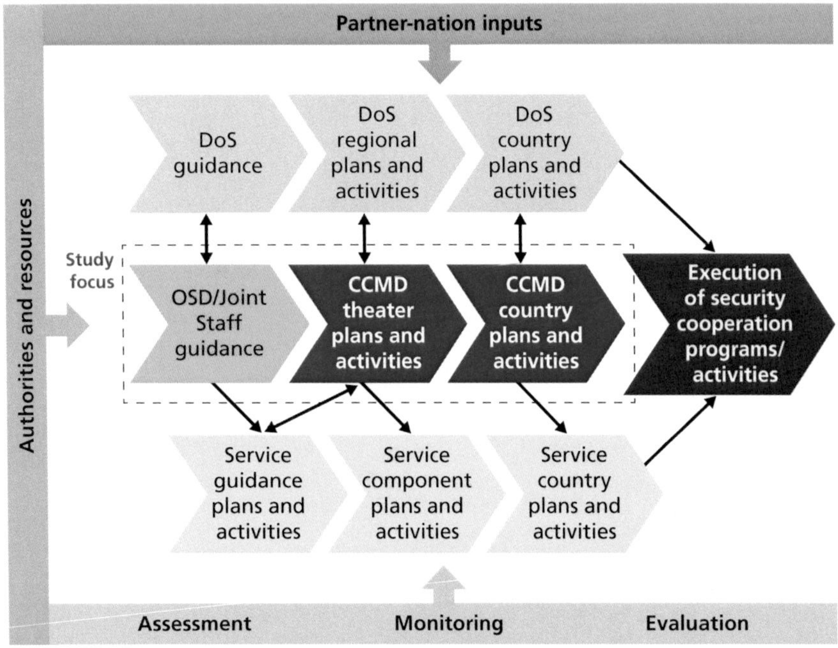

SOURCE: RAND analysis.
NOTE: DoS = U.S. Department of State.
RAND *RR1430-1.1*

and country plans. Finally, the content of all of these plans is affected by partner-nation requirements, the resources and authorities provided to conduct security cooperation activities, and evaluations of the performance, effectiveness, and efficiency of these activities.

Key Tasks

We undertook three tasks in support of OSD's efforts to overcome security cooperation planning and AME challenges through improved policy guidance.

Task 1: Analyze existing strategic-, operational-, and country-level security cooperation planning and AME practices and con-

nections. This involved conducting interviews with senior leaders, strategists, planners, programmers, assessors, and practitioners in OSD, the CCMDs, U.S. embassy–based security cooperation organizations (SCOs), and other government agencies to determine the extent to which they find security cooperation objectives appropriately specified, aligned, prioritized, and measured. We also discussed how stakeholders interpret security cooperation guidance, particularly whether it was sufficiently clear, detailed, and flexible.

Task 2: Develop and test a process for creating better security cooperation country objectives in cooperation with OSD and the CCMDs. OSD Policy staff provided sample security cooperation objectives extracted from CCMD planning documents to serve as prototypes for this exercise. Objective selection was complicated by the fact that each CCMD had a range of security cooperation–related intermediate military objectives and effects, lines of effort and activity, country end states, objectives and capabilities, and measures and indicators in their TCPs, country cooperation plans (CCPs), and CSCPs that more or less exhibited SMART characteristics. For our evaluation, we ultimately chose a set of current and approved statements for each selected country that we believed best expressed the command's security cooperation goals for the partner in the near to mid term. In U.S. Pacific Command's (PACOM's) case, this turned out to be country-related objectives compiled from various sections of the TCP by the J45 (Security Assistance and Cooperative Program Division). In U.S. Southern Command's (SOUTHCOM's) case, it was the intended effects of the command's TCP intermediate military objectives. In U.S. European Command's (EUCOM's) case, it was CCP lines of activity scoping statements. Finally, for our smaller U.S. Central Command (CENTCOM) analysis, we used security cooperation outcomes, which sit below the country objective level. Country objectives were very abstract goal statements that appeared not to be tailored to the country. The security cooperation outcomes were the highest-order country-specific statements we found.

These objectives were associated with 18 partner nations in four CCMDs: EUCOM, PACOM, SOUTHCOM, and CENTCOM.[3] We then analyzed the selected objectives according to well-recognized criteria from the goal-setting literature (described below) that we adapted for security cooperation purposes. Finally, in the cases of EUCOM, PACOM, and SOUTHCOM, we presented our evaluation of existing security cooperation objectives, along with illustrative alternative objectives, to CCMD country desk officers responsible for the selected partners. These experts provided feedback on our analysis, as well as their perspectives on country objective development.

Task 3: Recommend improvements to OSD security cooperation guidance and CCMD planning. Specifically, the RAND team was asked to suggests ways in which

- OSD Policy could better communicate its intent to CCMD security cooperation planners and resource providers
- CCMDs could improve their processes for developing country plan objectives using SMART criteria
- security cooperation staff could retain the skills necessary to develop and utilize SMART objectives.

Research Methods

To accomplish Task 1, we interviewed OSD and CCMD officials on country planning and AME practices, challenges, and remedies. To accomplish Task 2, we developed and applied a goal-setting tool derived from the business management literature (the RAND SMART

---

[3] Country selection was based on the assumption that cases should present a variety of situations that will be encountered by security cooperation staff, in order to provide maximum training value. Although the choice of partners was ultimately made by the CCMDs, we recommended the following selection criteria: the priority of the country to the CCMD, the focus of partner objectives (operational and institutional), political and security conditions in the country, and the quality of country objectives. Selected countries included Indonesia, the Philippines, Thailand, Sri Lanka, and Vietnam (PACOM); Georgia, Romania, Italy, Poland, and Moldova (EUCOM); Brazil, Chile, Guatemala, and Colombia (SOUTHCOM); and Armenia, Jordan, Turkmenistan, and the United Arab Emirates (CENTCOM).

objective framework) to a sample of objectives, and we held discussions with CCMD country desk officers on the utility and practicality of the framework's criteria. We then synthesized the results of the first two tasks to provide the evidentiary foundation for recommended changes to OSD security cooperation guidance and CCMD planning (i.e., Task 3).

Interviews with OSD and Global Combatant Command Officials

We conducted semistructured interviews in person and over the phone with DoD civilian and military officials in the Office of the Deputy Assistant Secretary of Defense for Security Cooperation and the Defense Security Cooperation Agency, as well as in the headquarters of the four CCMDs mentioned above. Study team members spoke to a range of senior leaders and staff officers engaged in theater campaign and security cooperation planning, programming, coordination, assessment, monitoring, and evaluation.

These interviews are attributed anonymously throughout the document in compliance with the U.S. Federal Policy for the Protection of Human Subjects (also known as the Common Rule). Both RAND's Institutional Review Board and human subjects protection reviewers within DoD approved of this research method for this study. Organizational affiliation is included in the citation for each anonymous interviewee to give a sense of the individual's background and experience, but interviewees were not asked to represent their organizations in a confidential way. While study subjects were asked to respond based on their professional experiences, they were in all cases speaking for themselves rather than for their organizations in an official capacity

RAND SMART Objective Framework

To meet our Task 2 goal of helping the CCMDs create better security cooperation country objectives for planning and AME purposes, we adapted and expanded a set of SMART goal-setting criteria that has been long employed by strategic planners in the business world and has been more recently used by DoD planners. As discussed earlier, the criteria for our SMART objective framework are that objectives be specific, measurable, achievable, relevant and results-oriented, and time-bound. To facilitate the application of these criteria to security cooperation planning, we expanded on this list of basic principles by adding the associated definitions and evaluation questions that are shown in Table 1.2.

Some SMART Caveats

While a useful planning device, the SMART construct should not be construed as the "be all and end all" tool for security cooperation objective developers. While the most popular, SMART is not the only recognized goal-setting framework.[4] In addition to its malleability, some SMART criteria can be ambiguous and/or situation-dependent, which is why we have attempted to clarify the elements of our construct. Also, SMART criteria can be in tension, if not actually conflicting. For example, an objective that is achievable by an executing agency may not be particularly relevant in terms of theater or national strategy and policy. Thus, obtaining a balance of SMART characteristics is generally preferred over an objective that is strongly weighted in favor of one or two elements. That said, in a complex organization, such as a CCMD, SMARTness rarely resides in a single planning objective; it is more likely to be found in different sections of a planning document or in multiple related planning documents. In particular, specificity regarding partner capabilities, timing, and responsibilities often increases as one moves from strategic guidance to implementation guidance. Finally, the utility of the SMART concept has been demonstrated largely through case studies rather than through quantitative social science techniques. Although there has been an increasing amount of solid research on goal-setting, there is little statistical evidence on the efficacy of the elements in the SMART framework (with the exception of specificity). Furthermore, this research has focused on individuals, not large organizations.[5]

---

[4] For example, other scholars have advocated for goals that have the following characteristics: specificity, proximity, hierarchical in organization, congruence, self-selected, consciously determined, learning-focused. See, for example, Dale H. Schunk and Barry Zimmerman, *Handbook of Self-Regulation of Learning and Performance*, Abingdon, UK: Routledge, 2011.

[5] Gary P. Latham and Gary A. Yukl, "A Review of Research on the Application of Goal Setting in Organizations," *Academy of Management Journal*, Vol. 18, No. 4, 1975.

Table 1.2
RAND SMART Objective Evaluation Framework

Criterion	Definition	Evaluation Questions
Specific	Objective is discrete; describes what is expected, by whom, and for/with whom	• Does the objective focus on a single intended outcome? • Does the objective indicate what specifically needs to be done? • Does the objective indicate who has the responsibility to help achieve the objective? • Does the objective indicate its principal target in the partner nation?
Measurable	Success is clearly and objectively defined; a regular, observable, objective, and sustainable method of measurement is in place	• Has a unit of measurement been established? • Has a baseline for measurement been established? • Does the objective indicate "how much" or "how many" units should increase or decrease? • Can U.S. government officials observe significant change from the baseline? • Is there a system in place to regularly and objectively monitor progress? • Is it sustainable?
Achievable	Requisite authorities, programs, and resources in place; partner-nation agreement secured; political and fiscal risks duly considered	• Do the authorities and programs exist to achieve the objective? • Are sufficient U.S. government resources likely? • Is there a way to overcome resource constraints? • Has the partner nation been consulted about how to achieve the objective? • If so, has the partner nation offered any resources (financial or otherwise)? • Does the partner nation have the capacity to absorb the U.S. government resources and programs required to achieve the objective?

Table 1.2—Continued

Criterion	Definition	Evaluation Questions
Relevant and results-oriented	Contributes to strategic goals; focused on significant partnership outcomes; prioritized and hierarchically organized	• Is the objective aligned with higher-level planning goals? • Is the objective nested within a hierarchy of objectives? • Is the objective challenging? • Is the objective framed in terms of partnership outcomes rather than process-level inputs or outputs?
Time-bound	Establishes a deadline or reasonable time frame for completion (generally, no more than five years)	• Is there a deadline or time frame for completion of the objective? • Is the deadline/time frame reasonable in terms of U.S. government priorities and available security cooperation resources? • Is the deadline/time frame five years or less?

At a minimum, what this means is that researchers and DoD planners should be cautious about applying SMART to security cooperation in a doctrinaire manner. The process of objective development is as much an art as a science. They should use their judgment as analysts and subject-matter experts to establish a sensible goal-setting framework that is guided but not determined by SMART criteria. It may be that certain criteria should not be applied to the same extent at every level of a planning hierarchy. Furthermore, there will often be a need to balance competing criteria, and this cannot be done in accordance with a predetermined formula. Finally, even though we have attempted to clarify SMART criteria by providing definitions and parsing them into narrower questions, we recognize that we have not eliminated subjectivity from the process of developing objectives. Although some of our questions can clearly be answered "yes" or "no," the answers to certain other questions depend on the opinions of those conducting the evaluation. Thus, we would recommend that two or more individuals, ideally from different organizations, independently evaluate each objective, and that they attempt to resolve any differences by consensus.

Application of the RAND Objective Framework

With the above caveats in mind, we undertook an initial evaluation of the selected partner-nation security cooperation objectives in the planning documents of several CCMDs. Based on our consultations with OSD, we chose to focus on select country objectives from EUCOM, PACOM, SOUTHCOM, and CENTCOM and then—given resource constraints—pursue in-depth interviews with staffs from EUCOM, PACOM, and SOUTHCOM.[6] Table 1.3 illustrates the results of this preliminary evaluation with respect to a single partner-nation objective in a single CCMD. If team members answered "yes" to a majority of applicable evaluation questions for a particular criterion, then the criterion was summarily evaluated as "satisfactory to good" and was color-coded green. If a majority of applicable evaluation questions were answered "no," then the criterion was evaluated as "unsatisfactory" and color-coded red. If there were an equal number of applicable "yes" and "no" responses, then the summary evaluation was "neither satisfactory nor unsatisfactory," and the criterion was color-coded yellow. In some cases, an evaluation question was determined "not applicable" (N/A) to a particular objective. For example, if a CCMD wanted to maintain some aspect of the partnership status quo indefinitely, then time-bound questions pertaining to the reasonableness or the length of an objective deadline would be "not applicable." In cases like this, the question was removed from the equation. For example, if a criterion (e.g., measurable) had six questions, and one was N/A and three of the remaining five questions were answered with a "yes," then that criterion for that objective was coded green. An assessment of the "achievable" criterion was not possible, due to insufficient information provided to indicate the security environment, political situation, or availability of U.S. forces to determine the achievability of a particular objective.

The full evaluation of our sample countries from EUCOM, PACOM, SOUTHCOM, and CENTCOM, including country names and objectives, is in the classified annex to this report.

---

[6] Based on discussions with OSD leaders and other stakeholders, we believe that the study team found a diverse mix of regions, countries, and objectives. We do not believe that a more extensive sample would have changed our key findings and recommendations.

Table 1.3
Illustrative Evaluation of a Partner-Nation Objective

Country	Objective	Evaluation Criteria	Evaluation Question	Evaluation Response	Summary Evaluation
A	1	Specific	Does the objective focus on a single intended outcome?	N	
A	1	Specific	Does the objective indicate what specifically needs to be done?	Y	
A	1	Specific	Does the objective indicate who in PACOM has the responsibility to help achieve the objective?	N	
A	1	Specific	Does the objective indicate its principal target in the partner nation?	N	
A	1	Measurable	Has a unit of measurement been established?	Y	
A	1	Measurable	Has a baseline for measurement been established?	N	
A	1	Measurable	Does the objective indicate "how much" or "how many" units should increase or decrease?	N	
A	1	Measurable	Can U.S. government officials observe significant change from the baseline?	N/A	
A	1	Measurable	Is there a system in place to regularly and objectively monitor progress?	Y	
A	1	Measurable	Is the monitoring system sustainable?	Y	
A	1	Achievable	Do the authorities and programs exist to achieve the objective?	?	

Table 1.3—Continued

Country	Objective	Evaluation Criteria	Evaluation Question	Evaluation Response	Summary Evaluation
A	1	Achievable	Are sufficient U.S. government resources likely?	?	
A	1	Achievable	Is there a way to overcome resource constraints?	?	
A	1	Achievable	Has the partner nation been consulted about how to achieve the objective?	?	
A	1	Achievable	If so, has the partner nation offered any resources (financial or otherwise)?	?	
A	1	Achievable	Does the partner nation have the capacity to absorb the U.S. government resources and programs required to achieve the objective?	?	
A	1	Relevant and results-oriented	Is the objective aligned with higher-level planning goals?	Y	
A	1	Relevant and results-oriented	Is the objective nested within a hierarchy of objectives?	Y	
A	1	Relevant and results-oriented	Is the objective challenging?	Y	
A	1	Relevant and results-oriented	Is the objective framed in terms of partnership outcomes rather than process inputs and outputs?	Y	
A	1	Time-bound	Is there a deadline or time frame for completion of the objective?	N	
A	1	Time-bound	Is the deadline/time frame reasonable in terms of U.S. government priorities and available security cooperation resources?	N/A	
A	1	Time-bound	Is the deadline/time frame five years or less?	N/A	

In addition to providing the CCMDs and OSD our initial evaluations of selected partner-nation objectives, we also sent them a list of objective alternatives based on the SMART criteria to facilitate discussions on improving the process of setting security cooperation goals. We then met with CCMD country desk officers in person or over the phone to discuss the ways in which our criteria were and were not useful for developing security cooperation objectives and the CCMD's requirements for establishing different kinds of objectives. We also discussed options for modifying the CCMD's goal-setting procedures in order to both satisfy their requirements and create "SMARTer" country objectives.

Organization of This Report

In Chapter Two, we place SMART objectives in the larger context of security cooperation planning and discuss additional considerations important to our analytic approach. Chapters Three through Five—focused on PACOM, EUCOM, and SOUTHCOM, respectively—are organized in a similar fashion: We begin with an analysis of existing theater campaign and country security cooperation planning and AME processes, including an account of process challenges and actual and potential responses to these challenges; we then describe our evaluation and revision of selected partner-nation objectives, along with CCMD perspectives on the SMART objective evaluation framework. In the final chapter, we summarize our cross-CCMD findings regarding country planning and AME processes. We also provide our recommended improvements to these processes and related OSD guidance.

CHAPTER TWO

Why Aren't SMART Objectives Enough?

When we began this study, we believed that setting SMART security cooperation objectives would inherently lead to improved security cooperation outcomes. While in some sense this is true, making the objectives SMART is itself a more complex process that requires the adoption of what can be thought of as a SMART *system*. In this chapter, we place SMART objectives into a larger, systemic context and begin to explore the major challenges involved in making security cooperation processes SMART.

SMART Objectives in Context

The SMART objective construct is a simplified extract of a much larger set of literature on goal-setting theory and management by objectives that spans both management and psychology.[1] While the first uses of the SMART criteria in academia appear to date from the 1980s, the conceptual origins are several decades older.[2] In 1954, Peter F. Drucker published a path-breaking work called *The Practice of Management*, in

[1] See, for example, the works of Edwin A. Locke, a preeminent researcher in the field, who taught across the fields of psychology and business. For example, Edwin A. Locke, Karyll N. Shaw, Lise M. Saari, and Gary P. Latham, "Goal Setting and Task Performance: 1969–1980," *Psychological Bulletin*, Vol. 90, No. 1, 1981.

[2] There is no consensus on who came up with the concept, but the earliest published record of the acronym appears to be George T. Doran, who labeled the letters specific, measurable, assignable, realistic, and time-related. See Doran, 1981.

which he argued that effective management paired setting of objectives at all levels with the ability for line managers to exercise what Drucker called self-control, but today would be more likely to be called ownership or self-determination.[3] Taken together, these elements of objective-setting and ownership are somewhat similar to the military doctrinal concept of mission command, according to which a commander sets forth a goal but gives the subordinate ownership over the means to pursue that goal, within specified limits. The concept applies more generally to civil-military command relationships, as well. In management, the process is somewhat more collaborative: Drucker argues that subordinates should set their own objectives, pending senior leader approval, and that higher management should help them to see both the big picture and the view from their own department.

A third element completes Drucker's analysis of the role of objectives in effective management. Measurement, or evaluation, provides the link between objectives and the individual's ability to determine his or her own path: "To control his own performance, a manager . . . must be able to measure his own performance and results against the goal."[4] Evaluation, for the benefit of oneself rather than one's superior, is thus the lynchpin of an effective goal-setting regime. This concept also resonates with established military strategic thought, particularly John Boyd's work on the observe-orient-decide-act loop, in which a constant feedback mechanism provides the "loop" that allows for effective decisionmaking throughout a changing situation.[5]

Our investigation of the context in which SMART objectives were developed helps us to uncover some necessary elements to be applied for successful SMART thinking: Objectives must be employed at multiple levels because organizations are hierarchical, objectives must be written by those who have ownership over the activities described, and evaluation must serve to enable managers to gauge their own progress

[3] Peter F. Drucker, *The Practice of Management*, New York: Harper & Row, 1954.

[4] Peter F. Drucker, *The Essential Drucker: Selections from the Management Works of Peter F. Drucker*, 1st ed., New York: HarperBusiness, 2001, pp. 120–121.

[5] John Boyd, *Science, Strategy and War: The Strategic Theory of John Boyd*, New York: Routledge, 2007.

toward these objectives. With this in mind, in the sphere of security cooperation, there are several common challenges or decision points that we found in the course of its research. The remaining sections discuss these decision points.

"SMARTness" of Higher-Level Guidance

As Drucker noted in his work on management by objectives, it is important that objectives exist at multiple levels. In fact, a higher-level SMART goal may be more likely to result in subordinate SMART objectives, because the subordinates can see clearly what outcome is expected by their superiors. Country security cooperation objectives are one level of guidance in a large and complex system. As the chapters of this report will describe in detail, the system as a whole extends from objectives listed in OSD planning guidance to the level of the individual event, incorporating guidance from CCMD commanders and, in a less formal sense, service and program objectives. These many objectives do not fully align with each other, meaning that the country-level objectives—where the rubber meets the road for putting dollars to activities in support of guidance—have to reconcile competing priorities. Often, these multiple perspectives on guidance are not written with SMART criteria in mind. As a notional example, the most recent national security strategy lists as a goal, "prevent the spread and use of weapons of mass destruction."[6] While the ensuing text goes into greater detail on how to pursue that goal, there is no discussion of how to measure progress, in what time frame success must be achieved, and which specific actors have responsibility for what portions of the activity. Of course, the national security strategy is written as an expression of the philosophy and guiding principles of a presidential administration more than as guidance, but it serves as a handy open source example for the reader to understand the form senior-level guidance often takes. Fundamentally, improving the SMARTness of country-

---

[6] The White House, *The National Security Strategy of the United States of America*, Washington, D.C., February 2015, p. 11.

level security cooperation objectives will be made easier by creation of a hierarchy of SMART objectives.

Top-Down Versus Bottom-Up Orientation

A top-down, or guidance-centric, view of security cooperation suggests that the "right" objectives will be those that best fit the total universe of prevailing guidance. But there is another view that is bottom-up, or country-centric. This viewpoint suggests that security cooperation can only be successful if the partner nation is a full and willing participant, and therefore that objectives must be written prioritizing those context-specific opportunities and activities, so long as they are resonant with the general goals of relationship-building.

Of course, good practice in security cooperation suggests that efforts are more successful when they align well with both donors' and partner nations' goals. This means that objective writers must find a way to reconcile both these top-down and bottom-up imperatives. In our research, the CCMDs tended toward one end of the spectrum or the other. For example, lessons from PACOM suggest drawing a more clear line from the objectives to OSD planning guidance, whereas for EUCOM, which has a strong top-down emphasis on alignment with guidance, it can be hard to ensure that objectives are specific and achievable. And in SOUTHCOM, where the objective-setting process has become highly centralized, there were concerns that objectives had become too specific and inflexible for implementers at the country level. There is no single answer to the question of what "right" looks like in this case, but as a general rule, CCMDs and OSD should be aware of this tension and of the need to find a balance that addresses these competing needs. Some sort of shared review of objectives, led either by the relevant CCMD or by OSD, could help resolve top-down versus bottom-up tensions and break down the stovepipes separating OSD, CCMD, and other stakeholders.

Who Writes the Objectives?

A related question concerns who is responsible for writing country-level security cooperation objectives: Are they written by CCMD staff, by senior defense officials (SDOs) in country, or someone else? In Drucker's argument, objectives should be written by the manager who will actually supervise the implementation of the activity, but in security cooperation, events require collaboration by many individuals who relate to each other nonhierarchically. In theory, an objective should be written by someone who has strong knowledge of the following:

- country context
- senior leader guidance
- security cooperation best practices
- subject matter relating to the security cooperation activity.

Thus, to write an objective relating to maritime interoperability activities in Romania, one would have to be familiar with Romania, EUCOM and OSD guidance for the region, training foreign forces, and naval operations. While some individuals may have expertise across several of these issues, it would be difficult to imagine a single person whose knowledge spanned all four areas. Thus, although we recommend that a single authority oversee objective development, the effort requires extensive coordination. We found no evidence of OSD or CCMDs conducting comprehensive reviews of objectives, despite general agreement among stakeholders that it was crucial to have a shared view of DoD's objectives on a country-by-country basis.

Each CCMD follows its own native process to complete the objectives. In SOUTHCOM, objectives are "owned" by intermediate military objective (IMO) integration managers, who are part of SOUTHCOM staff, but objectives require validation by security cooperation officers at the country level. At EUCOM, objectives are owned by offices of primary responsibility (OPRs), who are the functional experts for security cooperation activities. For example, in the maritime example above, the OPR could be U.S. Naval Forces, Europe, the EUCOM naval component; for a computer-related objective, the

OPR could be the J6 (Command, Control, Communications and Computers [C4]/Cyber Directorate) at EUCOM. Both EUCOM and SOUTHCOM have relatively function-centric approaches to objective writing. At PACOM, by contrast, the initial task of writing a country plan—and thereby objectives—is undertaken by the SCO/SDO, meaning that the PACOM process prioritizes country context in objectives, relative to other CCMDs. Of the four types of expertise listed above, it would be difficult to choose which should take priority; however, CCMDs and OSD should consider how the perspective of the primary objective author affects the substance of the resulting objective.

An additional consideration is the availability of time for objective development, particularly at PACOM and EUCOM, which have a broad range of non–security cooperation responsibilities. Writing security cooperation country objectives does not appear to be seen as a particularly prestigious activity in a time-constrained environment, possibly due to factors such as lack of socialization to their importance, lack of training, or lack of connection between achieving objectives and career success. If this is seen as problematic, solutions may lie in determining (1) what activities can be reallocated to allow objective writers to focus on the task, (2) who might have more time available for objective-setting, or (3) what can be done to elevate the perception of importance of this task in the eyes of those who must undertake it.

How Are Objective-Setting and AME Linked?

A final common decision point faced by CCMDs that affects the ability to generate SMART objectives is the linking of objective-setting with AME mechanisms. In fact, the system of AME is actually an integral part of the cycle of objective-setting over time. Weak AME mechanisms often mean that it is impossible to understand whether an objective has actually been achieved. This, in turn, weakens the entire objective-setting regime, making objectives and achievement less relevant. Each CCMD faces a decision point related to who conducts evaluations and what types of evaluation are undertaken. At EUCOM, for example, AME is qualitative and subjective, with narrative evaluations written by the same office writing the objective and signed off on by the SCO/SDO and country desk officer. In SOUTHCOM, due to a reduction in staff levels for evaluation, evaluation is conducted internally at several levels, including the SCO and IMO integration manager levels. At PACOM, the process is somewhat similar—narrative and qualitative—but the consultative process to determine evaluation results appears to incorporate more actors than simply those on the implementation team. A more indicator-driven approach is envisaged, combining both monitoring and evaluation data, but has yet to become reality. This indicator-driven approach should help to create unique measures for each objective that are set before implementation, holding programs to a more rigorous standard. Thus, most evaluations are qualitative, and while most tend to be internal, some tend to be more subjective than others. The principles of high-quality monitoring and evaluation are well known, and it is worthwhile for CCMDs to consider how these might be employed in security cooperation.

This leads to a subsequent question that the CCMDs must consider in security cooperation: How are objectives reviewed and revised? While country security cooperation plans may be revised from year to year, the strategic-level goals and lines of effort do not necessarily change on a yearly basis. While key goals persist, the "goalposts" may move from year to year, in recognition of the progress or lack thereof in achieving the previous year's objectives. This incorporation of evaluation and feedback into future goal-setting provides the "loop" in the observe-orient-decide-act loop. However, in the CCMDs we examined, it was difficult to understand whether and how feedback was incorporated into future objectives. For example, if an objective was not achieved and the efforts were not seen as a success, was the objective dropped from future plans? Was the objective altered so as to change the approach? Or was the timeline extended to allow the activity to continue another year? If the timeline is extended, how many extensions can be received before the activity is seen as a failure? There did not seem to be any clear process to feed the results of evaluation back into the objective-setting regimes, although this almost certainly happens on an ad hoc basis. CCMDs should be able to bring this critical information forward in a more structured way. One approach could be an after action report attached to the annual assessment process that provides a transparent and unvarnished explanation for the moving of goalposts, dropping or changing of objectives, etc.

Toward a SMART System for Setting Security Cooperation Objectives

While each CCMD has evolved different processes to set and evaluate security cooperation objectives, certain similar challenges must be overcome no matter what the context. It is also worth noting that the specific environment of security cooperation is made more complex by the fact that, although the CCMDs report to the Secretary of Defense, and the Deputy Assistant Secretary of Defense for Security Cooperation is in OSD, the CCMDs do not necessarily have a direct command relationship to a national policy–level organization for the purposes of security cooperation. So, while security cooperation objectives are hierarchically nested, there is not a single process for setting security cooperation objectives mandated by OSD for the CCMDs.

The focus of this report, however, is not so much on describing a single ideal process to be replicated by each CCMD. These are already strong institutions with long-established processes. Rather, our focus is on providing analysis and insights about the process of security cooperation objective-setting, as well as specific recommendations to improve processes in each CCMD.

CHAPTER THREE

PACOM Findings

PACOM security cooperation is capability-focused, as befits a CCMD whose chief goal is to ensure that the combined forces of the United States, its allies, and partners are ready to conduct a range of operations in the Pacific region against an array of threats, near- and long-term, natural and manmade. (Figure 3.1 shows PACOM's area of responsi-

Figure 3.1
U.S. Pacific Command Area of Responsibility

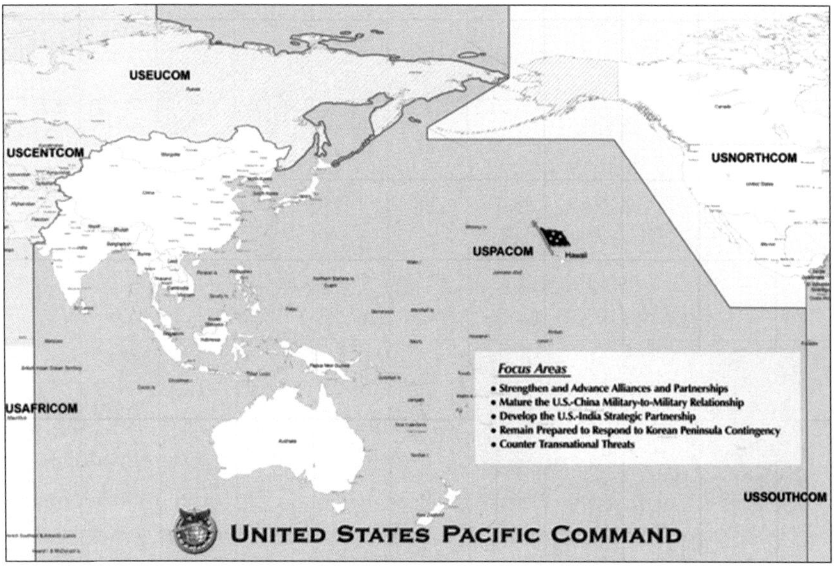

SOURCE: U.S. Pacific Command, website, no date.
RAND *RR1430-3.1*

bility.) Complicating PACOM security cooperation planning are the large numbers of military and civilian government stakeholders—in Honolulu, in Washington, D.C, in foreign capitals, and elsewhere—who must be consulted at various stages. Facilitating this difficult coordination task is a well-established battle rhythm that is administered by the PACOM J45 (Security Assistance and Cooperation Program Division) and includes two annual conferences in the spring and the fall that bring together all the major stakeholders in order to initiate and finalize the CSCPs developed primarily by the command's SCOs.

We begin this chapter with descriptions of PACOM's planning and AME processes for the theater campaign and partner-nation security cooperation and the nexus between them, based on interviews with responsible officials on the CCMD headquarter staff during the winter and spring of 2015. We then provide these individuals' perspectives on the challenges faced by planners, programmers, and assessors at each level and indicate what has been done or is being proposed to overcome these challenges. Next, we present our SMART-based evaluation of the security cooperation objectives for Indonesia, the Philippines, Sri Lanka, Thailand, and Vietnam that PACOM J45 provided to us in January 2015. This is followed by a summary of the feedback we received from PACOM country desk officers on our SMART objective development framework and illustrative alternative objectives during a visit to PACOM in April 2015. We conclude the chapter with our observations on the strengths and weaknesses of PACOM planning and assessment as they relate to the CSCPs.

CSCPs Are Part of a Complex Theater Planning Process

As Figure 3.2 indicates, there are a number of direct and indirect inputs to PACOM's CSCPs, which in turn influence other planning processes inside and outside the command. Shown at the top of the chart, OSD's planning guidance, which synthesizes Secretary of Defense–approved operational, posture, and security cooperation guidance for the CCMDs, military departments, and defense agencies, is the pri-

Figure 3.2
PACOM Country Security Cooperation Plan Inputs and Outputs

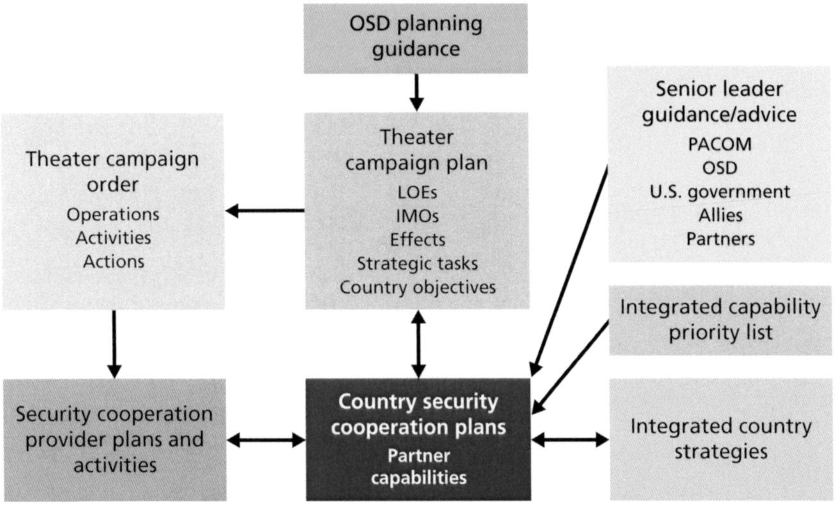

SOURCE: Authors' discussions with PACOM officials.
RAND *RR1430-3.2*

mary source document for the PACOM TCP.[1] OSD planning guidance provides campaign objectives for each CCMD (18 currently for PACOM)[2] and, according to PACOM officials, is used to develop and prioritize the command's lines of effort (LOEs) and IMOs.[3] Interviewees generally expressed satisfaction with OSD's 2015 planning guidance. Although they were somewhat critical of its task-orientation, they found it more prescriptive and practical than previous iterations.[4] Besides OSD planning guidance, PACOM planners make use of other

[1] Interview with PACOM headquarters official, phone interview with authors, February 20, 2015.

[2] Interview with PACOM headquarters official, phone interview with authors, February 10, 2015.

[3] Interview with PACOM headquarters official, phone interview with authors, February 20, 2015.

[4] Interview with PACOM headquarters official, phone interview with authors, February 20, 2015.

functional and regional strategy documents (e.g., related to countering weapons of mass destruction and improving maritime security) to refine IMOs and develop specific effects and tasks.[5]

The PACOM TCP looks out over a five-year period. (During the period of our study, J5 [Strategic Planning and Policy Directorate] planners were working on the FY 2016–2020 version of the document.) PACOM officials describe the plan as resource-informed, synchronized with DoD's budget cycle, and capable of being modified on an annual basis. They also indicated that the command had taken an "appetite suppressant" while developing the current TCP. Whereas the previous document was approximately 1,700 pages long and contained 170 IMOs, there are 38 IMOs in the current version, and supporting materials have been either excised or integrated into the main text, greatly reducing the length of the overall plan and, it is hoped, increasing its readability and usefulness to various customers. Interviewees emphasized that the current IMOs are not tasks but rather aspects of the regional environment that the command desired to realize by a specific date.[6] Furthermore, every component of the plan is prioritized, from LOEs to IMOs to effects to strategic tasks, based on OSD planning guidance.[7]

IMOs are bundled into 11 LOEs, which are identical to the 11 focus areas in the previous version of OSD planning guidance.[8] One of these LOEs, new to PACOM and eighth in terms of priority, is Allies and Partners. Along with the All Hazards LOE, it contains most of PACOM's security cooperation–related IMOs and effects. It should be noted, however, that the Allies and Partners LOE focuses on treaty allies and priority "emerging partners," which means that the majority

[5] Interview with PACOM headquarters official, phone interview with authors, February 20, 2015.

[6] Most PACOM IMOs are not country-specific, but there are exceptions.

[7] Interview with PACOM headquarters official, phone interview with authors, February 10, 2015.

[8] Interview with PACOM headquarters official, phone interview with authors, February 20, 2015.

of partner nations are not specifically addressed within the context of these LOEs.[9]

PACOM J5 country managers develop partner end states and objectives based on the LOE/IMO/effects roadmap, which are incorporated into country pages within the TCP.[10] Although they have not provided any formal goal-setting guidance or training, J5 regional division chiefs have advised country managers to rely on Joint Publication 5-0 (*Joint Operation Planning*) to help formulate their objectives and to focus their efforts on making their objectives condition-based, realistic, and in alignment with all relevant guidance.[11] Specificity and measurability appear to be of less interest to senior officials when it comes to country objectives.[12] In addition, during the previous iteration of the country planning process, the J5 and the J8 (Resources and Assessment Directorate) collaborated to provide country managers with a set of basic objective constructs (which managers were allowed to modify somewhat to account for particular national circumstances) that mirrored the IMOs and enabled the command to make cross-country comparisons.[13] Finally, PACOM uses security cooperation working groups and the staff coordination process to help refine proposed country objectives. Those involved in objective-vetting include representatives from various elements of the headquarters staff, as well as officials from the U.S. embassy and OSD.[14]

---

9 Interview with PACOM headquarters officials, in-person interview with authors, April 7, 2015.

10 Country pages are intended to address a range of issues of interest to PACOM, including security cooperation. They provide country end states and objectives that help guide security cooperation planning efforts at the country level. Interview with PACOM headquarters official, phone interview with authors, February 20, 2015.

11 Joint Publication 5-0, *Joint Operational Planning*, Washington, D.C.: Joint Chiefs of Staff, August 11, 2011.

12 Interview with PACOM headquarters official, phone interview with authors, February 20, 2015.

13 Interview with PACOM headquarters officials, in-person interview with authors, April 9, 2015.

14 Interview with PACOM headquarters official, phone interview with authors, February 13, 2015.

According to PACOM officials, the 2015 country objective development process will be more collaborative than heretofore. Rather than relying on country managers with limited regional and functional expertise to formulate objectives, LOE managers will direct a process involving multiple subject-matter experts from the headquarters staff, direct report units such as Joint Interagency Task Force West, security cooperation organizations, service components, and defense agencies.[15] In the meantime, however, country objectives seem to have been deemphasized as a factor in the development of CSCP capabilities, reportedly because SCO officials do not care for them.[16]

CSCPs Focus on Partner Capability Development

PACOM's CSCPs are intended to synchronize security cooperation ways and means employed by service components and other security cooperation providers with the objectives contained in the TCP, DoD's partner capability integrated priority list, and the U.S. embassies' integrated country strategies. Although PACOM J45 orchestrates the CSCP process in coordination with the J5, SCOs, who report to the PACOM commander and the U.S. ambassadors in their host nations, are responsible for writing the plans, with input from a number of sources.[17] According to one such official, the SCO's "mandate is very broad" and involves "translat[ing] various guidance into something that is executable."[18] In addition, SCOs are the primary vehicles for providing host-nation confirmation and ensuring that capabilities are

---

[15] Interview with PACOM headquarters official, phone interview with authors, February 13, 2015.

[16] Interview with PACOM headquarters officials, in-person interview with authors, April 8, 2015. Country objectives were not included in the draft CSCPs presented at the May 2015 PACOM Theater Security Cooperation Working Group meeting in Portland, Oregon (although country end states were included in these plans).

[17] Interview with PACOM headquarters official, phone interview with authors, February 19, 2015.

[18] PACOM Security Cooperation Office official, PACOM Theater Security Cooperation Working Group conference, May 12, 2015.

adequately resourced over a period of five years.[19] As a result, the partner capabilities described in the CSCPs are not always driven by an IMO in the TCP; sometimes an idea "bubbles up from the bottom" and a related IMO is subsequently developed.[20]

Aside from PACOM headquarters, the principal purveyors of guidance to the SCOs regarding the CSCP are OSD and the State Department. In particular, OSD has launched a new DoD initiative to develop a list of desired foreign partner military capabilities modeled on the CCMD's Integrated Priority List associated with the Joint Staff's Joint Capability Integration and Development System. According to PACOM officials, this foreign Integrated Priority List process should prove useful for obtaining security cooperation community agreement on contentious capabilities where there may be policy constraints and technological transfer issues, as well as for overcoming capability implementation and assessment challenges.[21] PACOM noted that synchronizing DoD and Department of State country security objectives has become easier in recent years. Consistent with the guidance provided by the April 2013 Presidential Policy Directive 23 (Security Sector Assistance), DoD representatives now have an important role in composing the security chapters of the U.S. embassies' integrated country strategies. One PACOM official indicated that he did not know of any partner nation where DoD and Department of State goals were not aligned, although he acknowledged that integrated country strategy goals are often stated very broadly.[22]

PACOM's annual CSCP battle rhythm starts in the fall, with the capability development working group. Its purposes include synchronizing country security activities, incorporating the partner-nation per-

[19] Interview with PACOM headquarters official, phone interview with authors, February 10, 2015.

[20] Interview with PACOM headquarters official, in-person interview with authors, April 8, 2015.

[21] Interview with PACOM headquarters official, in-person interview with authors, April 8, 2015.

[22] Interview with PACOM headquarters official, in-person interview with authors, April 8, 2015.

spective via the SCOs in the planning process, and providing direction to security cooperation providers on areas of special interest, whether that be counterterrorism, humanitarian assistance, maritime security, etc. In addition, PACOM senior leaders offer corrective guidance to the SCOs should any of their proposed "operations, activities, and actions" appear to be in conflict with CCMD objectives for the SCOs' region or country.[23] Following the capability development working group conference, SCO officials return to their posts, consult with their host-nation militaries on planned capability-oriented activities, work with the U.S. country team to integrate PACOM's country plan into the integrated country strategies, and secure the approval of the U.S. ambassador on the proposed capability roadmap. In the spring, SCO chiefs validate their draft CSCPs with senior leaders invited to PACOM's theater security cooperation working group conference. In addition to the PACOM J4 (Logistics, Engineering, and Security Cooperation Directorate) and J5, these leaders include representatives from OSD, the service headquarters, the defense agencies, and some of the United States' closest defense allies that, along with the United States, comprise the "Five Eyes" group (the United Kingdom, Canada, Australia, and New Zealand).[24]

The CSCPs presented at the May 2015 Theater Security Cooperation Working Group conference included five major elements: (1) country end states taken from the TCP, (2) priority LOEs, (3) prioritized capabilities and capacities, (4) an analysis of partner capability gaps, and (5) an "enduring employable capability roadmap." The final element was depicted as a graph with two axes—employable capabilities (y-axis) and partner readiness (x-axis)—and somewhat standardized partner capability building blocks displayed in a linear fashion, generally starting with develop (man, train, and equip) and proceeding to demonstrate (via exercises), refine (on the basis of after action reviews), realize (attain an initial capability), ensure (perhaps through

---

[23] Interview with PACOM headquarters official, phone interview with authors, February 20, 2015.

[24] Interview with PACOM headquarters official, phone interview with authors, February 20, 2015.

continued exercises), and enhance (take on a leading regional security role, for example).[25] According to PACOM officials, once these CSCP elements had been validated, they would constitute the basis for discussions with defense industry representatives, providing them with a clear idea of DoD strategic priorities in the PACOM region and letting them know what DoD is and is not likely to approve in terms of security assistance packages.[26] In addition, high-priority CSCP capabilities would be incorporated into Annex O (Security Cooperation) of the 2015 TCP, along with specific training, manning, and equipping actions.[27] In turn, these planned actions would be used as inputs to PACOM's annual theater campaign order—security cooperation is one of 12 joint mission-essential tasks—and the service component campaign support plans, which specify the operations, activities, and actions to be carried out by security cooperation providers.[28]

Security Cooperation AME Is Focused on the Allies and Partners Line of Effort

PACOM officials do not generally distinguish between assessment, monitoring, and evaluation and tend to combine these functions under the heading of assessment.[29] That said, PACOM's main AME focus is on evaluating the progress that the command is making with respect to the LOEs spelled out in its TCP. As Figure 3.3 attests, this LOE-based

---

[25] PACOM Theater Security Cooperation Working Group conference, May 13, 2015.

[26] Interview with PACOM headquarters official, phone interview with authors, February 19, 2015.

[27] Interview with PACOM headquarters official, in-person interview with authors, April 8, 2015.

[28] Interview with PACOM headquarters official, in-person interview with authors, April 8, 2015.

[29] One PACOM assessment expert we interviewed did distinguish between environmental assessments (focused on understanding the basic conditions that could have an impact on operations) and operational assessments (geared toward measuring the performance and effectiveness of operations). Interview with PACOM headquarters officials, in-person interview with authors, April 7, 2015.

Figure 3.3
PACOM's LOE Evaluation Framework

RAND *RR1430-3.3*

evaluation process is systematic and complex. Derived from OSD planning guidance campaign objectives, broadly stated but time-bound IMOs are subdivided into a number of more specific *effects,* which represent environmental conditions resulting from an action or actions that contribute to IMO achievement. Within the Allies and Partners LOE, the effect is usually the first level that may refer to a particular partner nation. Effects are evaluated by measures of effects, generally qualitative criteria, and associated quantitative metrics called MOE indicators. Effects are further broken down into *mission-essential tasks,* which constitute the basic steps required to achieve effects. These *strategic tasks* are evaluated by measures of performance, resources required for mission accomplishment, and capability enablers known as MOP indicators. Interviewees indicated that this evaluation process had not yet been fully exercised. At the time of the writing of this report, however, measures of effect and associated MOE indicators and measures of performance and associated MOP indicators were still under development, leaving the AME process for allies and partners incomplete.[30]

Within PACOM, LOE evaluation is conducted in three stages. In the first stage, members of the J83 (Strategic Assessments Division) and a varying number and type of subject-matter experts participate in strategic assessment working groups that evaluate IMOs and effects (currently) and measures and indicators (in the future). Depending on the LOE and the IMO being discussed, participating subject-matter experts may include country desk officers, current and future operations planners, and experts in special operations, weapons of mass destruction, and information operations, among others[31] Although J83 takes the lead in these working groups, the process is collaborative, and subject-matter experts must validate any assessment decisions.[32] At this point, TCP evaluators generally rely on proxy qualitative measures rather than direct quantitative measures—that is, they "stay away from math" when doing evaluations of IMOs, in particular, which are "too large to measure quantitatively."[33] The groups spend the majority of their time determining threshold criteria for red-yellow-green "stoplight" objective assessment charts. In addition to these summary evaluations, the J83 synthesizes subject-matter experts' comments in a narrative evaluation that includes justification for any changes in a rating. Although each objective evaluation is an aggregate of expert opinions, not everyone's vote is considered equal; the views of those

---

[30] Interview with PACOM headquarters officials, in-person interview with authors, April 7, 2015.

[31] Interview with PACOM headquarters officials, in-person interview with authors, April 7, 2015.

[32] Interview with PACOM headquarters officials, in-person interview with authors, April 7, 2015.

[33] Interview with PACOM headquarters officials, in-person interview with authors, April 7, 2015.

with greater expertise on a topic are weighted more heavily.[34] Once a strategic assessment working group has made an initial determination on progress on the IMOs in its LOE and provided a list of insights and recommendations stemming from its analysis, its evaluation product is reviewed, first, by PACOM's Joint Effects Validation Board, chaired by the J3 (Operations Directorate) and, second, by the Joint Effects Steering Board, chaired by the deputy commander.[35]

At present, TCP tasks are largely self-evaluated by those responsible for executing them. J83 does not view it as its responsibility to evaluate programs; rather, its prime goal is to ensure that activities are defensibly linked to the TCP. Accordingly, it was expected that in 2015 the J35 (Future Operations Division) would ask the service components to establish a clear linkage between their high-level "operations, actions, and activities" and PACOM's IMOs.[36] Although PACOM has considered using the evaluation portion of DoD's Global Theater Security Cooperation Management Information System (G-TSCMIS),[37] several officials expressed doubts regarding the comprehensiveness of its operations, actions, and activities entries and about the rigor and character of the evaluation questions, which incentivize security cooperation providers to positively evaluate their events.[38] While relying on G-TSCMIS to provide a common operating picture of security cooperation activities, PACOM has developed a separate web-based monitoring mechanism, the Strategic Management System, to keep track of

---

[34] Reportedly, PACOM J8 has sent requests for information to the SCOs to add country-level input to the evaluation of certain IMOs within the Allies and Partners LOE, but this interaction has not worked as well as expected. Interview with PACOM headquarters officials, in-person interview with authors, April 7, 2015.

[35] Interview with PACOM headquarters officials, in-person interview with authors, April 7, 2015.

[36] Interview with PACOM headquarters officials, in-person interview with authors, April 7, 2015.

[37] G-TSCMIS is an event-level DoD database that is intended to permit members of the security cooperation community to plan, monitor, and analyze the full range of security cooperation activities, programs, and resources.

[38] Interview with PACOM headquarters officials, in-person interview with authors, April 7, 2015.

LOE objectives, effects, tasks, and measures, as well as the results of its LOE evaluations.[39]

The AME process associated with the CSCP is less structured and mature than the theater campaign process, with its framework of objectives, effects, measures and indicators, evaluation working groups, and information management system. SCOs are largely responsible for assessing partner-nation needs and evaluating progress in filling capability gaps.[40] PACOM J4 and J5 leaders and other security cooperation stakeholders review their determinations at the annual PACOM Theater Security Cooperation Working Group conference. In addition, J5 regional division chiefs reportedly discuss the performance of security cooperation activities with their partner-nation counterparts on a regular basis.[41] Although there is currently no explicit connection between the theater and country AME processes, it is possible that country-oriented IMO effects could provide such a linkage, though only for high-priority partners.

The Planning Process Does Not Explicitly Link Security Cooperation Ends, Ways, and Means

PACOM's complex and transitional planning and assessment processes pose challenges for planners, programmers, and AME experts, including those involved in country objective development. Some interviewees at PACOM headquarters complained there were more LOEs than staff personnel to adequately cover them. Others felt there were too many elements in the TCP structure; in particular, the rationale for having measures of effects/measures of performance and MOE/MOP indicators was not clear to them. Still others questioned what they saw as an imbalance between planning and AME focused on partner capa-

---

[39] Interview with PACOM headquarters officials, in-person interview with authors, April 7, 2015.

[40] Interview with PACOM headquarters official, phone interview with authors, February 20, 2015.

[41] PACOM Theater Security Cooperation Working Group conference, May 13, 2015.

bilities as opposed to partners' willingness to engage with the United States.[42] AME experts, in particular, noted that PACOM objectives and activities were more implicitly than explicitly aligned[43] and that legacy activities were at times "backward engineered" so they appeared to flow from existing IMOs.[44] A unique problem for security cooperation officials is the structural difference between CCMD and Department of State planning, with the former oriented on LOEs and the latter being country-centric.[45] We found it difficult to determine what should be the unit of analysis for our security cooperation objective improvement task, given the range of "objective-like" planning elements at PACOM (IMOs, effects, measures, indicators, country end states, country objectives, and partner capabilities), as well as the variety of opinions on their significance and need for SMARTness.[46] In sum, despite its recent streamlining, PACOM's complex planning process does not explicitly link strategic and theater level "ends," security cooperation and other "ways" of achieving these ends, and the programmatic and personnel "means" associated with these ways. A simpler system, whose elements are collectively if not individually SMART, could benefit PACOM officials charged with campaign and security cooperation planning, programming, and assessment, as well as policymakers in Honolulu and Washington who must make the case that the resources provided to DoD are being used for the purposes for which they were intended.

Another challenge for country-level planning at PACOM is the variance in the abilities and responsibilities of J5 country managers,

---

[42] Interviews with PACOM headquarters officials, phone interviews with authors, February 20, 2015.

[43] Interview with PACOM headquarters officials, in-person interview with authors, April 7, 2015.

[44] Interview with PACOM headquarters officials, in-person interview with authors, April 7, 2015.

[45] Interview with PACOM headquarters officials, in-person interview with authors, April 7, 2015.

[46] Interviews with PACOM headquarters official, in-person interview with authors, April 8, and 9, 2015; PACOM headquarters official, PACOM Theater Security Cooperation Working Group conference, May 12, 2015.

who have traditionally been responsible for developing country end states and objectives. According to PACOM officials, these personnel are not trained as planners and do not always see the utility in laying out a roadmap for U.S. engagement with partner nations. Many have little time for long-term planning activities, such as a mission analysis of country objectives, because they are focused on current operations, such as managing senior leader engagements.[47] Furthermore, country managers have until recently worked in relative isolation on country objective development. As a result, country objectives have often been both insufficiently detailed and redundant.[48]

Country planning has also suffered from inadequate partner-nation input. Because of classification restrictions, PACOM officials can in some cases discuss objectives tangentially, but not the timeline for their accomplishment.[49] With respect to certain objectives, they cannot talk to partner nations at all.[50] In a few cases (e.g., Australia), CSCPs are being written bilaterally. That said, partner nations are involved early on in capability planning. Although PACOM initially proposes a combination of desired capabilities, officials claim they are willing to consider changes if a partner wants something different. However, they are somewhat leery of acceding to partner requests, finding that partner nations often "attempt to push above their weight"—for example, by attempting to build special operations capabilities. Also, partners pose challenges because of their different cultural practices and interests and their ability to pit the United States against its competitors in

---

[47] Interview with PACOM headquarters official, phone interview with authors, February 20, 2015.

[48] Interview with PACOM headquarters official, phone interview with authors, February 19, 2015.

[49] Interview with PACOM headquarters official, phone interview with authors, April 13, 2015.

[50] Interview with PACOM headquarters official, in-person interview with authors, April 8, 2015.

the "phase zero space." In the end, PACOM officials say, they are "not in the business of providing everybody what they want."[51]

AME present its own set of challenges for security cooperation objective developers at PACOM. Many evaluations are being conducted at a fairly high level, leading to a lack of emphasis on the level between the operations, actions, and activities and the IMOs—that is, between the effect or the country objective, depending on whether one is referring to the TCP or the CSCP.[52] Also, important stakeholders are involved in some AME processes but not others. According to PACOM headquarters officials, it is difficult to persuade busy SCOs to participate in TCP LOE evaluation, as they see little advantage to doing so.[53] For its part, PACOM J83 has no role in evaluating CSCPs.[54] Finally, there is no event in PACOM's battle rhythm at which the entire staff conducts a full-fledged baseline assessment of a partner nation—in terms of capability development, key leader events, and training and exercises. This is understandable, however. Recently, when PACOM J5 directed a "deep dive" assessment of a single country (the Philippines), it took many members of the command staff and subject-matter experts from outside PACOM over a hundred hours to complete. One interviewee questioned whether this process was replicable for more than a handful of priority countries.[55]

PACOM Is Taking Steps to Mitigate Planning and AME Challenges

PACOM has undertaken or is considering a number of steps to mitigate some of the planning and AME challenges described above. To

---

[51] Interview with PACOM headquarters official, phone interview with authors, February 10, 2015.

[52] Interview with PACOM headquarters official, in-person interview with authors, April 8, 2015.

[53] Interview with PACOM headquarters officials, in-person interview with authors, April 7, 2015.

[54] Interview with PACOM headquarters official, in-person interview with authors, April 8, 2015.

[55] Interview with PACOM headquarters officials, in-person interview with authors, April 7, 2015.

increase accountability and improve the alignment of ends and means, PACOM will begin to directly assign military activities for a two-year period via the theater campaign order to specific command components starting in FY 2017; it will require all component activities to be related to CCMD objectives.[56] To help address the issue of inexperienced and overtasked country managers, PACOM J5 is adopting a team approach to developing country pages that will give functional and regional specialists more of a role in goal-setting.[57] Greater expert input into this process could enable PACOM to modify its rather formulaic country objective development method, which has resulted in nearly identical objectives being applied to many partners, seemingly without regard to their capabilities, absorptive capacity, or willingness to engage in a particular area.[58] There is also recognition among senior officials of the need to incorporate the partner-nation perspective into PACOM planning, not to drive strategy but to inform capability development—in particular, to better understand where the command has a reasonable chance to succeed and where it does not.[59] To overcome partner-related challenges, some favor enhancing the power of SCOs in country planning.[60] Others think that formal OSD country guidance could be helpful if it could be used to communicate to partners DoD's major capability priorities and if the CCMDs were included in the drafting process.[61] According to PACOM planners, reducing the number of IMOs and making them more directive and time-bound will improve

---

[56] Interview with PACOM headquarters official, phone interview with authors, February 20, 2015.

[57] Interview with PACOM headquarters official, phone interview with authors, February 13, 2015; interview with PACOM headquarters officials, in-person interview with authors, April 9, 2015.

[58] Interview with PACOM headquarters officials, in-person interview with authors, April 9, 2015.

[59] Interview with PACOM headquarters official, in-person interview with authors, April 8, 2015.

[60] Interview with PACOM headquarters official, phone interview with authors, February 19, 2015.

[61] Interview with PACOM headquarters official, phone interview with authors, February 13, 2015.

the assessment process by allowing staff to focus limited resources on a clearly defined set of issues.[62] In the future, PACOM is planning to assess discrete capabilities in individual countries using detailed mission-essential task criteria.[63] Some officials would also like to provide security cooperation executors with a checklist of what is needed to complete specified tasks in order to better monitor developments in partner nations.[64] Potentially, J83 could pull this information into PACOM's Strategic Management System to inform campaign evaluation via an improved G-TSCMIS evaluation mechanism that indicated the purpose of the task, what had been achieved, and how the task was linked to CCMD IMOs and effects.[65]

RAND Evaluation and Revision of Selected Partner-Nation Objectives

After gaining an appreciation for PACOM's planning and AME processes and the challenges faced by process implementers, RAND study team members conducted an initial SMART evaluation of the country objectives of five partner nations (Indonesia, the Philippines, Sri Lanka, Thailand, and Vietnam), as laid out in Tab A to Appendix 8 to Annex C to USPACOM TCP 5000-20 MOD 1. Compiled by the PACOM J45 and J5 staffs, this tab reportedly contained the most recent (as of January 2015) CCMD country-level security cooperation guidance. Along with the country end states and objectives, mainly developed by PACOM J5 country managers, Tab A listed proposed

---

[62] Interview with PACOM headquarters official, phone interview with authors, February 20, 2015.

[63] Interview with PACOM headquarters official, phone interview with authors, February 20, 2015.

[64] Interview with PACOM headquarters official, in-person interview with authors, April 8, 2015.

[65] Interview with PACOM headquarters official, in-person interview with authors, April 8, 2015.

country capabilities and strategic communications themes, which were intended to be used as inputs to CSCPs.

A caveat before summarizing the results of our country objective evaluation: The objectives we scrutinized could be characterized to a certain extent as "straw men." In other words, the objectives themselves do not appear to be an important factor in current security cooperation planning. Furthermore, PACOM J5 officials have advised SCOs to turn their attention to IMOs, rather than existing country-level end states or objectives, when devising their CSCPs.[66] Having said this, we contend that our PACOM objective exercise was valuable, because the strengths and weaknesses identified in these examples would apply to any PACOM objective development effort. Directly associating security cooperation activities with partner nations to mostly regional IMOs can obscure the connection between ends and means, because IMOs are broadly written and do not generally indicate what is expected in terms of specific changes at the country level. At some point, PACOM will need to fill the gap with explicit partner milestones, whether it calls them country objectives or IMO effects or something else. And these objectives should be as SMART as makes sense in terms of who is being engaged, what is being done, and how it is being done.

Security Cooperation Objectives Are Insufficiently Specific, Measurable, and Time-Bound

Although the SMARTness of existing PACOM security cooperation objectives varies considerably, we observed some general trends in the extent to which the command's country objectives are in line with SMART criteria.[67] Table 3.1 summarizes these trends.

---

[66] PACOM headquarters official, PACOM Theater Security Cooperation Working Group conference, May 12, 2015.

[67] See the appendix for a detailed evaluation of the security cooperation objectives of our five selected countries by country and objective. For classification reasons, partner names and objective wording have been left off this evaluation.

Table 3.1
PACOM Initial Country Objectives Evaluation

SMART Criterion	Evaluation
Specific	• The majority of the objectives we examined were rated as unsatisfactory for this criterion (red); almost all of the remainder were rated neither satisfactory nor unsatisfactory (yellow). • Many objectives were focused on multiple outcomes; some were specific about what needed to be accomplished, and some were not. • Most objectives did not indicate which organization within PACOM or the partner-nation military was primarily responsible or which were the major coordinating agencies inside and outside DoD.
Measurable	• About 60% of the objectives were rated unsatisfactory (red); the rest were rated satisfactory to good (green). • Although objectives often established at least a qualitative unit of measure, frequently they did not provide a baseline for measurement or indicate "how much" or "how many" units should be increased or decreased. • It was also unclear in many cases whether there was a system in place to regularly, objectively, and sustainably monitor progress toward achieving the objective.
Achievable	• This criterion was not assessable because our source document (TCP Tab A) did not contain an environmental or risk assessment that examined such factors as the partner's willingness to help achieve the objective or the level and availability of resources required to achieve the objective (gray). • Some of the above factors are considered within the context of PACOM's capability development working group and theater security cooperation working group; however, the results of working group exchanges regarding the achievability of security cooperation objectives are not currently captured in a formal written document.
Relevant and results-oriented	• All the objectives were rated satisfactory to good (green). • Most country objectives appear to conform to higher-level guidance; however, it was not always clear whether a particular objective should be a priority for a particular country.
Time-bound	• Over 50% of the objectives were rated unsatisfactory (red), and almost 40% were rated satisfactory to good (green), which indicates that PACOM has not standardized the application of this criterion. • This criterion did not apply to a few objectives that called for maintaining a condition at a certain level.

SOURCE: RAND analysis.

Examples Provided on Ways to Make Objectives SMARTer

After conducting our initial SMART evaluation, we created alternative illustrative objectives that added certain details to the essential content of existing country objectives based on the requirements of the SMART framework and other relevant information, such as the capabilities associated with the country objectives in Tab A. Notwithstanding our limited subject-matter expertise, these illustrative alternatives provided a concrete point of departure for our discussions with PACOM country desk officers on the desired characteristics of country objectives and the utility of the SMART framework for objective development.

Although most of the 40 PACOM country objectives we reviewed are classified, Table 3.2 demonstrates our objective revision process using an unclassified objective for an unnamed selected partner nation. This country objective is not intended to be representative of the full set of existing objectives, but it does reveal several of the weaknesses mentioned in the previously described SMART evaluation summary: a lack of specificity, measurability, and time-boundness. As the center column of the table notes, the objective has two aims rather than a single clear goal. It is not clear to what extent the partner should adhere to the United Nations Convention on the Law of the Sea or by what

Table 3.2
Sample Revision of Selected Partner-Nation Objective

Existing Country Security Cooperation Objective	SMART Critique	Revised Objective
Country X adheres to established norms of conduct and agrees to a common understanding of the rights as set forth in the United Nations Convention on the Law of the Sea (UNCLOS). Country X has the capacity and will to provide multilateral maritime security and uphold norms of conduct.	• Compound objective. • To what extent will Country X adhere to UNCLOS? • By when? • How will Country X demonstrate maritime security will and capacity? • By when? • With which multilateral partners? • Responsible security cooperation parties?	1. Country X navy refrains from firing at unarmed fishing vessels in the Y Strait in 2016 (Navy component in coordination with the U.S. embassy). 2. In 2017, Country X navy hosts a regional conference of law of sea experts to discuss ways to peacefully resolve boundary disputes in the Z Bay (Navy component in coordination with the U.S. embassy).

dates it needs to demonstrate its adherence. How and when is the country meant to demonstrate its will to provide maritime security, and with which multilateral partners? Who at PACOM and in the partner nation should be held responsible for achieving this dual objective? The right-hand column attempts to illustrate how one might correct these flaws by splitting the existing objective into two and specifying who in the partner nation should do what by when, to assess its adherence to UNCLOS and its willingness to contribute to maritime security in its region. It also specifies which CCMD organization should be primarily responsible for assisting the partner nation to achieve the revised objectives and with which interagency partner it should coordinate.

Perspectives on the SMART Framework Varied

PACOM perspectives on RAND's SMART framework and its application to selected partner-nation security cooperation objectives varied somewhat. At the leadership level, there was substantial support and appreciation for the goal of improving country objectives. Also, some desk officers indicated that our list of illustrative alternative objectives provided a concrete template for setting country goals that might compensate for the limited guidance and training they had received on composing country objectives.[68] However, some resisted the idea of making country objectives more specific, measurable, accountable, and time-bound. They preferred keeping objectives related to U.S. military access to partner nations as "gray" as possible, believing that the specifics of any agreements were subject to change, especially during a crisis, and to a large extent outside PACOM's ability to control. Furthermore, they were inclined to defer to SCOs and service components on the particulars of building partner capabilities because of their greater subject-matter expertise and to let them establish partner readiness requirements and security cooperation responsibilities in their plans, instead of including these elements in the TCP country objectives. Finally, the interviewees were reluctant to establish firm dates for objective accomplishment. The political environment, they contended, sometimes con-

---

[68] Interview with PACOM headquarters officials, in-person interview with authors, April 9, 2015.

strains the ability to achieve objectives, and the dates associated with some existing objectives seemed aspirational or arbitrary.[69] Also, one senior PACOM official saw value in increasing the specificity of TCP objectives but "not at the expense of realism."[70] Another did not see a reason to change PACOM's current process of writing, staffing, and reviewing country objectives. Although acknowledging that the process had received some criticism from assessment personnel, he believed that planning should drive assessment, not the reverse.[71]

Conclusion

PACOM officials are generally confident that their command is on the right track with respect to TCP and security cooperation planning and AME. In particular, they believe that the 2015 TCP—thanks in part to the revised theater guidance contained in the recent OSD planning guidance—will be a more comprehensible and assessable document than the previous version. PACOM also has a well-developed, although perhaps overly complex, framework for evaluating the IMOs associated with its major LOEs, which now include allies and prioritized emerging partners. Furthermore, PACOM's process of bringing together all the key security cooperation stakeholders in biannual working groups focused on partner capability development is a potential model for all the CCMDs. Yet, in spite of the close relationship between senior officials in the J5 and J45, the connection between theater and country planning and AME is not as tight as it could be. One reason for this is the lack of well-accepted country objectives to guide security cooperation planning and help ensure the alignment of security cooperation ends, ways, and means. Most PACOM officials acknowledge that

---

[69] Interview with PACOM headquarters officials, in-person interview with authors, April 9, 2015.

[70] Interview with PACOM headquarters official, phone interview with authors, February 13, 2015.

[71] Interview with PACOM headquarters official, phone interview with authors, February 13, 2015.

existing country objectives are not specific or realistic enough to serve this purpose, and they believe that RAND's SMART framework could help to resolve their planning dilemma.

Another recognized shortcoming is the security cooperation AME process. Aside from the lack of sustained attention from PACOM's AME experts, this process also suffers from the paucity of SMART country objectives that link desired changes in partner conditions to PACOM approved activities. Fortunately, the SCOs' capability development roadmaps (which include periodic exercises and after action reports) may provide the foundation on which to build an AME process. But PACOM will still need to develop AME roles and responsibilities, performance and effectiveness measures, and a system for sharing, managing, and analyzing security cooperation data. Presumably, G-TSCMIS could be part of the solution if its evaluation module were upgraded. But something more customized will probably be needed to monitor progress toward the achievement of tasks and milestones along each country capability LOE.

CHAPTER FOUR

EUCOM Findings

The security cooperation process at EUCOM is robust and complex, characterized by unique processes and systems. This complexity presents a number of challenges for clear objective-setting, largely due to the time required to synchronize all players. While the evaluation process is similarly well developed, the analysis is driven by self-assessment. In this chapter, we describe EUCOM's planning and assessment processes for its TCP and security cooperation activities with partner nations and the role of objectives in those processes, drawing mainly on interviews with responsible officials on the CCMD headquarters staff. Next, we review the challenges associated with these processes. We then provide our evaluation of security cooperation objectives for a select set of countries based on SMART criteria. These countries were selected in conjunction with OSD and EUCOM, in order to have regional variation across the CCMD, as well as across a spectrum of higher- and lower-capability partner nations. Following this, we summarize the feedback we received from EUCOM headquarters staff on the objective development framework and our illustrative alternative objectives during a visit to EUCOM in May 2015. Finally, we provide concluding thoughts on the planning and assessment process and on the feasibility of improving the adherence of EUCOM's security cooperation objectives to the SMART framework.

Figure 4.1 shows the EUCOM area of operations.

Figure 4.1
EUCOM Area of Operations

SOURCE: U.S. European Command, website, no date.
RAND *RR1430-4.1*

Planning Processes Are Multilayered and Complex

The EUCOM process for security cooperation planning is detailed, with an emphasis on aligning the various strata of security cooperation–related guidance. In the following section, we summarize the portions of the EUCOM planning cycle that are relevant to security cooperation.

Synchronizing Strategic and Operational Guidance Is a Major Task

As Figure 4.2 demonstrates, the top-most level of guidance for security cooperation is found in the OSD planning guidance objectives, as

Figure 4.2
Simplified EUCOM Theater Campaign Framework

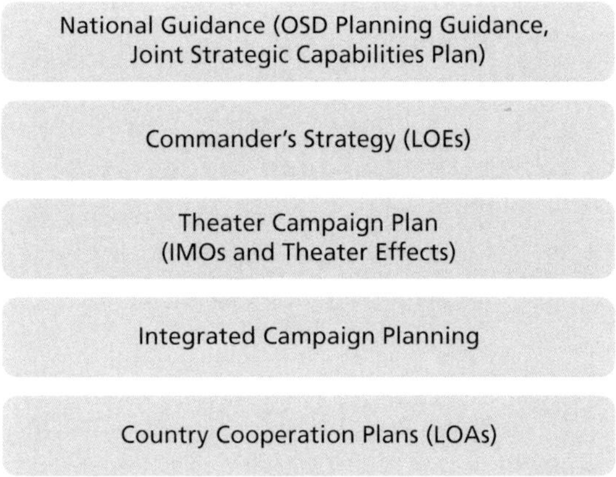

SOURCE: Rich Guffey and Jim Welton, "Strategy-to-Task Implementation Through Country Cooperation Plans and Lines of Activity," EUCOM briefing document, May 13, 2015, p. 4.
RAND *RR1430-4.2*

well as in the Joint Strategic Capabilities Plan. At the CCMD level, the commander has priorities that are in accord with, but derived separately from, OSD planning guidance. These are expressed in LOEs that transcend individual countries in the theater. Beneath this level is the TCP, which unifies OSD planning guidance and commander's strategy and generates IMOs. Other integrated campaign plans, such as plans for EUCOM's two geographic subregions or for specific issues, such as cybersecurity, exist below that level and are built based on the IMOs.

It is at the level of the CCP that the varying levels and types of guidance are harmonized. CCPs look out between two and five years, and translate guidance into action. The CCP operationalizes the commander's LOEs, each of which contains one or more lines of activity (LOAs), which typically reference IMO and OSD planning guidance objectives in their rationales. Thus, it can be said that the backbone for an LOA is the commander's guidance, but that national and other guidance function as supporting elements to drive LOAs.

At EUCOM, one somewhat unique complicating factor is the prioritization of NATO goals and the difficulty of synchronizing and prioritizing NATO objectives with all the forms of guidance discussed in Figure 4.2. NATO objectives do make an appearance in the CCPs, and often they do relate to the commander's strategy and TCP. But it is a challenge for EUCOM staff to synchronize the specific language and to incorporate NATO goals into the prioritization process.[1] To some degree, this happens obliquely, in that the strategic value calculation, which we describe below, weights the commander's strategy heavily, and this can be shaped by NATO's priorities, but the process is informal.

The development cycle for plans begins in March with the EUCOM Strategy Conference and Workshop, described by staff as the "Burning Man of security cooperation."[2] This is a very large conference, at which a wide variety of stakeholders gather to learn what is happening in the region. The conference covers a wide range of security cooperation events and strategies, including, for example, discussion of NATO plans.[3]

Through June, staff take the direction provided by the conference and refine it to generate an LOA task order, which directs the completion of activities.[4] Plans are then updated between June and September, and in October feedback is solicited from the country team, along with an assessment of the resource needs required to complete the activities.[5] In December, the EUCOM Strategy Implementation Conference

---

[1] Interview with EUCOM headquarters officials, in-person interview with author, May 12, 2015.

[2] Interview with EUCOM headquarters officials, in-person interview with author, May 12, 2015. "Burning Man" is a large festival in the Nevada desert and here is used to signify a large, multi-event confabulation that attracts a variety of participants.

[3] Walter L. Perry, Stuart E. Johnson, Stephanie Pezard, Gillian S. Oak, David Stebbins, and Chaoling Feng, *Defense Institution Building: An Assessment*, Santa Monica, Calif.: RAND Corporation, RR-1176-OSD, 2016, p. 90.

[4] Robert L. Kloecker, "Implementing the Commander's Strategy: Theater Campaign Framework," May 12, 2015, p. 5.

[5] Interview with EUCOM headquarters officials, in-person interview with author, May 12, 2015.

reviews the previous fiscal year, resources are matched to new activities, and an execution program is developed for the new fiscal year.[6] Between the EUCOM Strategy Implementation Conference and the next year's EUCOM Strategy Conference and Workshop, plans from the OSD level down to the CCP are updated as necessary, and the effort begins anew.[7]

Country Security Cooperation Objective-Setting Involves Many Actors

The LOA level is the fulcrum of EUCOM's security cooperation work and the key level of focus for this study. This is in possible contrast to other CCMDs, such as SOUTHCOM, where the IMO appears to fill this function. EUCOM maintains a standard portfolio of 45 LOAs to be used in the CCPs.[8] As seen in Figure 4.3, the LOE represents a broad goal, whereas an LOA is a specific action to be taken. However, the standard LOA is still too generic to drive effective implementation of objectives by a country team.

To drive security cooperation events, the LOAs must be customized to reflect country-specific goals and realities. This happens through a process that is unique to EUCOM—the drafting of an LOA scoping statement that serves as the actual country-level security cooperation objective. The scoping statements are written by a trio of actors described below, led by the OPR, which comprises the functional specialists for the work. The OPR may be a section at EUCOM, such as the J5/8 (Policy, Strategy, Partnering and Capabilities Directorate) or J6 (Command, Control, Communications and Computers [C4]/Cyber Directorate), or it may be the component, such as U.S. Army Europe or U.S. Naval Forces, Europe. While the OPR retains the responsibility for drafting the scoping statement, the other two parties who review it are the SCO/SDO and EUCOM country desk officer. The three repre-

---

6 Kloecker, 2015, p. 5.

7 Kloecker, 2015, p. 5.

8 Interview with EUCOM headquarters officials, in-person interview with author, May 12, 2015.

Figure 4.3
Sample Linkages Between Strategy and Tasks

SOURCE: Guffey and Welton, 2015, p. 8.
RAND *RR1430-4.3*

sentatives must arrive at consensus on the objective.[9] Within EUCOM, awareness of the SMART construct is high, and the staff who manage the plans process within the J5/8 do so with awareness of SMART principles. For example, the sample LOA scoping statement used in EUCOM briefings reads, "The BGR [Bulgarian] 61st MECH BDE [mechanical brigade] is deployable and interoperable at battalion level with US BCTs [brigade combat teams] and NATO units."[10] This statement, along with the implied LOA timeline of three to five years and the more specific nested outcomes to be discussed below, constitutes a SMART security cooperation objective according to the definition set forth in this report.

Within EUCOM, the number of LOAs generated may be exceedingly high, and not all are of equal priority. To establish some form of prioritization, EUCOM's J5/8 Research and Analysis Division devises a composite measure, which gives 35 percent weight to an LOA's OSD

---

[9] Interview with EUCOM headquarters officials, in-person interview with author, May 13, 2015.

[10] Kloecker, 2015, p. 9.

planning guidance objective priority, 40 percent weight to the CCMD commander's priority, and 25 percent to the functional area proponent's priority (functional areas include, for example, health services or explosive ordnance disposal). Collectively this provides "a relative measure of conformity to senior leader direction."[11]

Information Management

Another unique part of EUCOM's security cooperation process is its use of SAS Plan, a database interface developed by EUCOM's J5/8 Research and Analysis Division to manage security cooperation activities.[12] However, SAS Plan has a greater level of detail than static security cooperation planning outputs; it is a live repository for security cooperation that is more detailed than what appears in either the CCP or the CCP roadmap document, the version of the LOEs and LOAs that is releasable to partner-nation governments. SAS Plan contains not only the scoping statements but also outcomes, which describe "what must be true to accomplish this result [in the LOA scoping statement]."[13] Finally, SAS Plan holds records of tasks and events that support the intended outcome. This system has some functional overlap with the G-TSCMIS; however, in discussing the G-TSCMIS system, staff commented that it was too complex and not user-friendly. For example, one respondent commented that recording an event in G-TSCMIS requires staff to know the Treasury code for the funding, information the person entering the data seldom has.[14] Further, SAS Plan appears to have greater utility as a planning tool—serving as the repository for security cooperation objectives and plans—while G-TSCMIS is more focused on event tracking and monitoring.

---

[11] Kloecker, 2015, p. 9.

[12] *SAS Plan* initially stood for "Strategy for Active Security Plan"; however, that term is no longer in use.

[13] ECJ5 Research and Analysis Division, untitled SAS Plan instructional document, April 29, 2015.

[14] Interview with EUCOM headquarters officials, in-person interview with author, May 13, 2015.

Evaluation Data Are Largely Self-Assessment

The EUCOM security cooperation assessment process also begins with SAS Plan and the generation of an LOA progress report. The LOA progress report is a narrative and largely subjective look at progress toward the LOA scoping statement goals, although it contains color-coded assessments, with green meaning on track, yellow meaning off track but results still achievable, and red meaning off track.[15] The narrative portion of the progress report includes sections for current status, results, hindrances to accomplishment, and strategy and plan considerations.[16] While the progress report is written by the OPR, it is reviewed by the U.S. embassy's SDO and signed off on by the EUCOM country desk officer.[17] The progress reports are generated on a yearlong cycle, with Black Sea/Eurasia reports due in the first quarter, Southeast Europe reports due in the second quarter, Central Europe reports in the third quarter, and Western Europe reports due in the fourth quarter.

The primary purpose of AME at EUCOM is to support EUCOM's work and to inform the commander. The process is viewed as geared more toward EUCOM interest than OSD interests, as it focuses more narrowly on output measures rather than impact.[18] Once the progress reports have been generated in SAS Plan, they are integrated by J7 (Exercises and Assessments Directorate) into country assessments and thematic assessments. These higher-level evaluations combine the LOA progress reports with political and military analysis.

In addition to this level of assessment, EUCOM J7 also prepares the comprehensive joint assessment for EUCOM, part of a common process across the CCMDs to assess progress toward OSD planning

---

[15] Interview with EUCOM headquarters officials, in-person interview with author, May 13, 2015.

[16] Perry et al., 2016, p. 133.

[17] Interview with EUCOM headquarters officials, in-person interview with author, May 13, 2015.

[18] Interview with EUCOM headquarters officials, in-person interview with author, May 13, 2015.

guidance objectives and IMOs.[19] This assessment contains sections relating to the assessment of the strategic environment, concept plan and operation plan assessment, and drivers of risk. The audience for this joint assessment is Washington, in particular, the Joint Staff.

Planning and Assessment Face Several Challenges

While the EUCOM planning and assessment process is highly developed, it does have several shortcomings, often resulting from the complexity of the process. While understanding of SMART objectives is high at EUCOM, many LOA scoping statements are not expressed as SMART objectives. In part, this is due to the number of actors involved in the process, with the OPR, SDO/ODC, and country desk officers all involved in objective-setting. The process is collaborative, but at no time in the process are the three stakeholders in a room to decide what direction to pursue with activities and what resources and activities are needed to purse it.[20] While the OPRs retain primary responsibility for the objective-writing and assessment process, they are functional experts in the subjects to be covered by security cooperation activities, such as cyber defense or civil affairs, rather than experts in either security cooperation or the country itself. The country desk officers at EUCOM, meanwhile, were described by respondents as overcommitted with tasks such as preparing briefing books; moreover, these positions are often staffed by National Guard augmentees, who were described as not having adequate backgrounds in security cooperation or the partner nations.[21]

A related challenge is that SAS Plan is difficult for implementers to use, or, as one respondent said, "we see SAS Plan as disconnected

---

[19] Interview with EUCOM headquarters officials, in-person interview with author, May 13, 2015.

[20] Interview with EUCOM headquarters officials, in-person interview with author, May 12, 2015.

[21] Interview with EUCOM headquarters officials, in-person interview with author, May 12, 2015.

from reality."[22] Because the database holds the dynamic, "living" versions of the security cooperation goals and activities, it is important that it be accessible and useful to EUCOM's many security cooperation stakeholders. Yet, since SAS Plan is maintained on a classified network, it can be difficult for SDOs and other embassy staff to access the information it contains.[23] In addition, because the LOA process begins in earnest in August, when many embassy staff are arriving at or leaving their posts, it can be difficult to engage them in the objective-setting process.[24]

The LOA scoping statement is therefore plagued by a combination of lack of experience, lack of time, and lack of access to the system. There is oversight of the process, and there is an available PowerPoint document that describes the difference between weak and strong, or SMART and less SMART, objectives, but the EUCOM staff we spoke with did not feel that this document was broadly utilized. Figure 4.4 presents a version of EUCOM's training materials for authors of LOA scoping statements. It articulates attributes of SMART and non-SMART statements, using the fictional country of Bandaria in its examples. However, the total number of unique scoping statements numbers around 640, which makes quality assurance difficult with a small and busy staff.[25]

The result of these procedural barriers to SMART objective-writing is that LOA scoping statements often fall far short in SMARTness. In a demonstration of SAS Plan for the RAND team, scoping statements varied widely in quality, and some replicated the definition statement for the standard LOA, with almost no customization for the country. Moreover, it was unclear how often the LOA scoping

---

[22] Interview with EUCOM headquarters officials, in-person interview with author, May 13, 2015.

[23] Interview with EUCOM headquarters officials, in-person interview with author, May 12, 2015.

[24] Interview with EUCOM headquarters officials, in-person interview with author, May 13, 2015.

[25] Interview with EUCOM headquarters officials, in-person interview with author, May 13, 2015.

Figure 4.4
Sample Guidance on LOA Scoping Statement Development

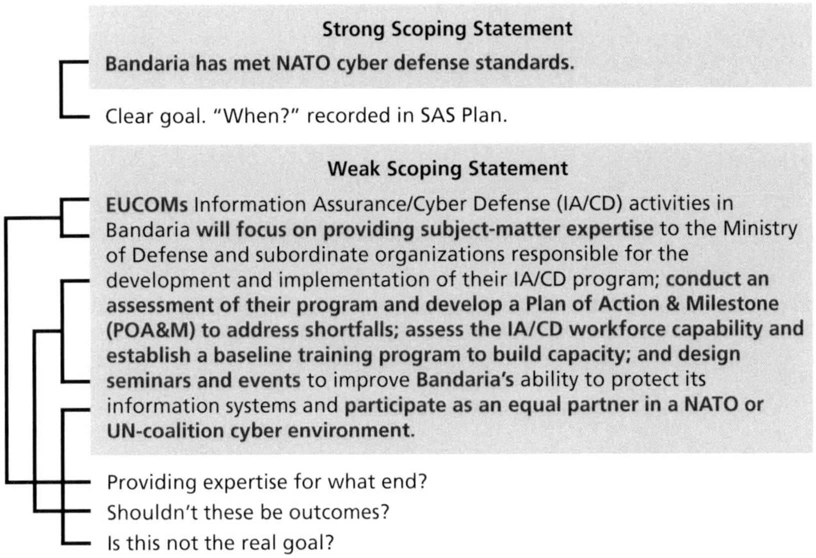

SOURCE: U.S. European Command ECJ5 Research and Analysis Division, untitled SAS Plan training document, April 29, 2015.
NOTE: Highlights in text from original, for the purpose of emphasizing which elements are being addressed by the specific comments in the graphic.
RAND *RR1430-4.4*

statements changed, and what led to changes.[26] LOA scoping statements have an implied horizon of three to five years, but it is unclear whether failure to make progress would result in a poor assessment of progress or in rescoping of the LOA statement to reset the time frame. One respondent reported that the result was that U.S. embassy country teams simply decided what they wanted to do and found an LOA that would fit.[27]

Another respondent commented that LOA progress reports are capable of delivering the right information if the scoping statements

---

[26] Interview with EUCOM headquarters officials, in-person interview with author, May 13, 2015.

[27] Interview with EUCOM headquarters officials, in-person interview with author, May 13, 2015.

are well written and the progress reports are filled out thoroughly and clearly.[28] Staff noted that these are "plans-based" assessments, meaning they assess progress against completion of planned activities (i.e., outputs), rather than serving as an impact (i.e., outcome) assessment. The assessment has a narrow scope, apparently because EUCOM staff feel this helps to constrain the subjectivity of the assessor. While the EUCOM strategy of assessing progress against planned outcomes has validity according to our assessment, if the objective itself is poorly written, an effective assessment is unlikely. Moreover, the person writing the progress report may or may not be the person who designed the LOA or implemented the activities.[29]

Therefore, the progress reports themselves will necessarily vary in quality. If the assessments are poor quality, the people revising plans will not use them, and it will become increasingly hard to determine whether engagements are making progress against objectives.[30] Given that assessments are annual but the horizon of the LOA scoping statement is three to five years, should EUCOM staff rewrite the scoping statements every year in order to look an additional three years in the future, or should they hold the objectives constant until the end of the time window? Either of these could be a rational approach, but the guidance must be clear and the approach documented.

An important critique of EUCOM's process was provided by a staff member who felt that the process as a whole had become overly top-down and hierarchical, and thus "detached from reality."[31] This staffer went on to say that, when each subsequent level is simply the rote, disaggregated version of the level immediately higher, there is a false presumption that achieving the lower-level objective will auto-

[28] Interview with EUCOM headquarters officials, in-person interview with author, May 13, 2015.

[29] Interview with EUCOM headquarters officials, in-person interview with author, May 13, 2015.

[30] Interview with EUCOM headquarters officials, in-person interview with author, May 13, 2015.

[31] Interview with EUCOM headquarters officials, in-person interview with author, May 12, 2015.

matically equate to achieving the higher-level objective.[32] This staffer felt that an approach that focused more closely on country-level influence-mapping would have both greater fidelity to country-level needs and connection to the ultimate goals of the OSD planning guidance.[33] Such an approach would entail identifying risks that would endanger U.S. security objectives in a country and opportunities to influence those risks positively.

Proposed New Changes Fix Some, but Not All, Issues

EUCOM staff are in the process of addressing several of the areas of concern raised in this chapter. For example, when this report was being written, EUCOM had plans to host a series of meetings in fall 2015 for security cooperation stakeholders for each country. These meetings would allow the actors involved to meet face-to-face to plan for security cooperation and discuss resources.[34] Further, EUCOM officials noted they are increasing access to SAS Plan at the country-team level.[35] Finally, EUCOM staff have developed revised guidance on preparing LOAs and LOA scoping statements to sharpen their focus on SMART objectives.[36] However, the process for assessing progress toward security cooperation objectives remains a complex one that may not be perfectly suited to implementation in a diverse, distributed environment.

---

[32] Interview with EUCOM headquarters officials, in-person interview with author, May 12, 2015.

[33] Interview with EUCOM headquarters officials, in-person interview with author, May 13, 2015.

[34] Interview with EUCOM headquarters officials, in-person interview with author, May 13, 2015.

[35] Interview with EUCOM headquarters officials, in-person interview with author, May 12, 2015.

[36] Communication with EUCOM headquarters official, email discussion with author, September 10, 2015.

RAND Evaluation and Revision of Selected Partner-Nation Objectives

The RAND team, in conjunction with staff at OSD and EUCOM, selected five EUCOM countries for more detailed analysis of security cooperation objectives. Georgia, Italy, Moldova, Poland, and Romania, were selected to cover a broad range of security cooperation "postures," from highly capable partner nations where activities tend toward interoperability exercises, to less-capable countries with a fuller suite of security cooperation activities.[37] We considered the LOA scoping statements to be the security cooperation objectives for the purpose of this study. EUCOM maintains these statements in the "roadmap" annex to each country's CCP, as well as in SAS Plan.

As with the other CCMDs studied, we conducted an initial evaluation of the objectives, scoring each objective on the presence or absence of SMART attributes. As discussed above, we used as country-level objectives the LOA scoping statements written by the OPRs, country desk officers, and SCO/SDOs. For EUCOM, because of the very high number of unique LOA scoping statements, we selected five representative unclassified objectives from each of the five selected countries. Following this analysis, we selected a subset of these objectives, two per country, for which to develop illustrative SMART objectives based on the previously written security cooperation objectives. While we do not have the country-level expertise to draft security cooperation objectives for EUCOM's staff, this exercise was intended to generate discussion about how the existing objectives can be written more concretely, rather than to add new security cooperation goals for EUCOM. A detailed evaluation of the security cooperation objectives of our five selected countries, by country and objective, can be found in the appendix. For classification reasons, partner names and objective wording have been left out of this evaluation.

---

[37] Interview with EUCOM headquarters officials, in-person interview with author, May 13, 2015.

Initial SMART Evaluation Shows Varied Results

As should now be clear, security cooperation objectives have a variety of authors, depending on the subject matter and partner nation under discussion. Thus, there are many different approaches to the writing of objectives and significant variation in SMARTness. However, some trends did become apparent in analyzing the selected EUCOM security cooperation objectives. Objectives rated poorly for measurability, and many were written in such a way that units of measurement would be difficult to develop. EUCOM's objectives scored well on relevance/results-orientation, in part because of the nested hierarchical structure of objectives for that scoring, but in part because EUCOM objective writers excelled at expressing goals in terms of partner-nation outcomes. For the most part, objectives were not time-bound, because they lacked clear deadlines by which to gauge success. Table 4.1 details these trends.

Illustrative Objective Revision Focuses on Measurement and Time-Bounding

Table 4.2 shows a sample objective, along with a short critique and an illustrative revision that shows how the objective could be rewritten to be more aligned with SMART principles.

EUCOM Staff Advocated That SMART Framework Emphasize Authorities, Risk

We attempted to use our illustrative objectives to generate a discussion about improving fidelity to SMART guidelines. However, training on SMART principles at EUCOM did not seem to be the deficiency, as already discussed. In fact, when we brought out our illustrative objectives worksheet, a EUCOM staff member brought out a worksheet that was structured very similarly. However, EUCOM staff indicated that the objectives assessment worksheet would be useful to the quality control of the LOA scoping statements, which appears to be the more vulnerable part of the objective-setting process.

The staff at EUCOM offered several useful critiques of the SMART framework. They recommended that the achievability section of the framework stress not only feasibility but also complexity

Table 4.1
Initial EUCOM Country Objectives Evaluation

SMART Criterion	Evaluation
Specific	• Objective ratings for specificity were mixed, with an equal number (40%) categorized as satisfactory (green) and neither satisfactory nor unsatisfactory (yellow), and a minority (20%) categorized as unsatisfactory (red). • There was no single pattern for the answers to the four subsidiary questions making up the specificity category of our SMART framework. In some cases, the objective focused on multiple outcomes; in others, the objective provided no indication of what needed to be done to achieve the objective. • Many objectives did not specify who within EUCOM or the partner nation was responsible for working to achieve the desired end state. While the OPR is designated with responsibility for the LOA, it is not clear that the OPR is responsible for engaging with the partner nation or carrying out the subsidiary activities.
Measurable	• Nearly all objectives were rated unsatisfactory (red) for this criterion. Only one of the 25 objectives was considered satisfactory (green). • In many cases, it was not possible to determine a unit of measurement, particularly for "maintenance" objectives, such as those seeking to maintain access to facilities. • Other objectives, such as assisting the country to develop a type of plan, have little in the way of easily discernible intermediate measures. It may be that for this type of effect, some common definition of intermediate steps is required.
Achievable	• Achievability was difficult to discern in the context of LOA scoping statements. • Subsidiary questions under the achievability category of our SMART framework asked whether authorities and funding existed from the United States or partner nation to implement this LOA, but while EUCOM staff indicated that LOAs may be assigned absent available funds, it is unclear in the CCP which objectives are unfunded.[a] • Another subsidiary question asked whether the partner nation had the ability to absorb the resources and programs offered. Here again, it was difficult to establish either a yes or no answer based on the information within the CCP or an understanding of the typical LOA scoping statement process.
Relevant and results-oriented	• All of the objectives we reviewed were rated satisfactory (green) for this criterion. • These questions focused primarily on alignment with higher-level goals. In some cases, the LOA scoping statements contained explicit references to alignment with integrated country strategies and other strategic documents. • One area in which EUCOM staff excelled was in framing these objectives in terms of partnership outcomes, rather than inputs and outputs. • One subsidiary question in this section that was sometimes difficult to answer was whether the objective is considered challenging to accomplish. In some cases, the objectives were ones that would be challenging for any country with average capabilities to develop within a three- to five-year time line.

Table 4.1—Continued

SMART Criterion	Evaluation
Time-bound	• Approximately 80% the objectives studied were rated unsatisfactory (red) for this criterion. In subsequent discussion with EUCOM staff, it was discovered that LOA scoping statements have an implied horizon of three to five years. However, it remains the case that only about 20% of cases dealt with time or deadline-setting explicitly, and the high degree of variability between three or five years for the remaining objectives makes it hard to consider them time-bound or scoped with direct reference to the partner nation's circumstances.

SOURCE: RAND analysis.

[a] Interview with EUCOM headquarters officials, in-person interview with author, May 13, 2015.

Table 4.2
Sample Revision of Selected Partner-Nation Objective

Existing Country Security Cooperation Objective	SMART Critique	Revised Objective
Combined Maritime Interoperability, Deployability, and Standardization (OPR: U.S. 6th Fleet). Focused on assisting the partner navy to improve its ability to conduct out-of-area operations and security assistance by ensuring it is trained to NATO standards for deployable harbor protection, improving interoperability, and developing capabilities.	• By when? • How will it be measured? • Does a good job of explaining what the United States will do. • Does a pretty good job of framing in terms of host-nation objectives.	By 2020, working with U.S. 6th Fleet, the partner navy will be able to conduct out-of-area operations and security assistance, as measured by its achievement of NATO standards in deployable harbor protection.

of authorities and availability of funds for the activity, as these are a key constraint on what can be done.[38] Staff cited a case they called the "house of cards," in which a complex system of authorities had to be cobbled together for an activity, but it was so precarious that the activ-

[38] Interview with EUCOM headquarters officials, in-person interview with author, May 12, 2015.

ity fell apart when one funding source did not come through.[39] This is also described as a "patchwork" of authorities. This indicates that it is not simply a question of whether authorities are available, but whether they are easily used and whether there are sufficient resources.

Another important critique made by EUCOM staff was that being time-bound may not be useful to every security cooperation goal, and non-time-bound measures with a clear and specific effect may suffice.[40] Incorporating this into the RAND SMART assessment framework is somewhat complex. One the one hand, it is true that certain security cooperation goals may not be easily sequenced in time, but on the other, an actionable plan to achieve an objective must be built with some cognizance of time and some way to tell whether the effort is excessive or the goal unattainable.

In several instances, EUCOM staff indicated that OSD could play a more productive role in the security cooperation objective-setting and assessment process. First, EUCOM staff noted that it would be helpful if OSD planning guidance objectives were framed in a way that was more in line with SMART principles, rather than what are perceived to be discrete tasks.[41] Second, staff noted that OSD did not ask for much in the way of information about security cooperation activities, and that the most helpful question OSD could ask would be "*Why* do you think your security cooperation activities are working or not working?"[42] While respondents did not specify when and how it would be appropriate to ask this question, the feeling appeared to be that asking a question like this would help to draw the focus of attention to the impact level of evaluation, rather than simply the output level. Finally, staff noted that the issue was not simply at the LOA scop-

---

[39] Interview with EUCOM headquarters officials, in-person interview with author, May 12, 2015.

[40] Interview with EUCOM headquarters officials, in-person interview with author, May 12, 2015.

[41] Interview with EUCOM headquarters officials, in-person interview with author, May 12, 2015.

[42] Interview with EUCOM headquarters officials, in-person interview with author, May 13, 2015.

ing statement level but that EUCOM plans generally could be better aligned with SMART principles at all levels.[43]

Conclusion

The case of EUCOM's objective-setting process highlights the need to view SMART objectives in the broader context of a SMART system. Elements of the SMART framework can be specified outside the language of the objective, as where the LOAs have an implied time horizon, so long as that is clearly specified. Equally, though, a simpler and SMARTer system at multiple levels of planning could provide better guidance and a better structure to provide relevant assessments up to higher echelons.

EUCOM officials have a highly developed system that connects multiple levels and types of guidance, as well as a custom-designed system to manage security cooperation efforts. However, this system is complex and very top-down-oriented, which means it may not actually be used as effectively as officials hope. While one solution might be to increase the personnel assigned to related tasks, another would be to simplify the system and create more opportunities for bottom-up or nonhierarchical contributions to planning. For example, SCO/SDOs, rather than the OPRs, could take responsibility for the initial drafts of the LOA scoping statements, in an attempt to make the objectives more tied to current conditions on the ground. This could also contribute to systems for more meaningful assessment by creating more relevant security cooperation objectives that country-level contributors to the assessment are more motivated to thoroughly assess.

EUCOM's process for security cooperation objective-setting and assessment is mature and serves the key tasks of harmonizing guidance and contributing to feeding into the resourcing functions well. Understanding of SMART framework criteria is high, and, with key process improvements, security cooperation objectives can be brought in line

---

[43] Interview with EUCOM headquarters officials, in-person interview with author, May 13, 2015.

with SMART principles, which should result in improvements to the activity-planning and assessment functions within EUCOM.

CHAPTER FIVE

SOUTHCOM Findings

Security cooperation is the central focus for SOUTHCOM's TCP, and, accordingly, there is negligible separation of security cooperation concerns from the remainder of SOUTHCOM's activities. The majority of planning is concentrated on steady-state activities to deter potential adversaries and support partner nations. While this allows a more focused approach to synchronizing activities horizontally and vertically within the CCMD, SOUTHCOM faces several challenges due to personnel cuts and a resource-constrained environment. As such, SOUTHCOM continues to refine its planning process to enhance synchronization, but lags in its ability to comprehensively assess achievement of its stated objectives.

In this chapter, we first describe the overall planning process for the development of SOUTHCOM's TCP and CCPs, based on interviews conducted with relevant officials from the headquarters staff and SCOs. Next, we discuss the strengths and weaknesses of the current system and detail some of the challenges faced by personnel at the CCMD and with the SCOs. Then, we present a synopsis of our initial evaluation of country security cooperation objectives for Brazil, Chile, Colombia, and Guatemala that OSD developed in fall 2014. Finally, we conclude with a holistic assessment of SOUTHCOM's objectives, based on current planning processes.

TCP Development Process Balances Strategic Guidance with Country-Level Reality

SOUTHCOM's security cooperation planning process is designed to effectively synchronize, deconflict, prioritize, and resource activities at the country level to ensure achievement of strategic objectives. SOUTHCOM predominantly focuses on "phase zero," or steady-state, activities; as one SOUTHCOM official commented, "SOUTHCOM has been doing security cooperation in the area of responsibility since [the Panama Canal]."[1] It is incumbent on the CCMD to thoroughly align its activities to support national guidance for the region as efficiently as possible in an especially resource-constrained environment. Linking of activities to national guidance is the organizing function for much of the TCP review process.

SOUTHCOM Guidance Focuses on Security Cooperation

The TCP operationalizes SOUTHCOM's strategy for achieving the assigned end states promulgated by OSD planning guidance by aligning subordinate objectives to directly connect country-level activities with strategic guidance. SOUTHCOM's approach to aligning programs with strategic guidance has been to develop a structure that centers on IMOs as the focal point around which security cooperation is planned, executed, and evaluated, and these are binned within general categories or LOEs. In 2015, SOUTHCOM had six theater-wide LOEs and 72 IMOs. Of note, SOUTHCOM divides the theater into four regions—the Caribbean, Central America, Andean Ridge, and Southern Cone—and the TCP prioritizes LOEs within each region, which in turn prioritizes IMOs. Below the IMO level are the country-level objectives that increase in specificity from *effects*, down to *specified tasks*, *milestones*, and *targeted capabilities*, with each level adding greater specificity. While the last three categories were dropped from the TCP later in 2015, they are still part of objectives and AME design.

Figure 5.1 shows SOUTHCOM's area of responsibility.

---

[1] Interview with SOUTHCOM official, May 19, 2015.

Figure 5.1
SOUTHCOM Area of Responsibility

SOURCE: U.S Southern Command, website, no date.
RAND *RR1430-5.1*

It is important to note that SOUTHCOM, unlike other CCMDs, does not have a separate Security Cooperation Annex to its TCP, because it considers all activities as security cooperation–related. Instead, SOUTHCOM has developed a synchronization product, which it calls the Phase Zero Nesting Model, to more clearly show linkages and alignment between OSD planning guidance end states and activities executed at the country level, across the SOUTHCOM enterprise, and to provide greater clarity of guidance to subordinate commands.[2] This nesting model is an Excel spreadsheet that serves as the central planning and coordination instrument and had, until early 2015, included in the TCP the entire hierarchy of objectives from the theater-level LOEs down to country-level targeted capabilities. However, this planning product was seen as unwieldy and too specific for a strategic-level document.[3] Accordingly, the country-level specified tasks, milestones, and targeted capabilities were removed from the TCP and managed at the implementation (i.e., SCO) level. Thus, the TCP maintains a higher-level focus, and SCOs are given greater flexibility in designing their implementation plans while maintaining a system that documents security cooperation objectives with extensive detail. The nesting model is reviewed from the SCO up to the SOUTHCOM commander and assigns OPRs and supporting organizations to oversee the achievement of the assigned objectives to ensure that guidance is clearly linked and in alignment with OSD planning guidance end states and SOUTHCOM LOEs.

Figure 5.2 shows the major components and stakeholders of SOUTHCOM's theater security cooperation development process.

SOUTHCOM Nests Objectives Within the TCP

The TCP process begins in August with an initial build of higher-level objectives, led by IMO integration managers. Using internal partner assessments, monitoring tools, and evaluations, these managers solicit inputs from CCMDs and SOUTHCOM directorates to draft initial IMOs and effects. This hierarchy is then sent to the SCOs, who review

---

[2] Interview with SOUTHCOM official, May 19, 2015.

[3] Interview with SOUTHCOM official, September 30, 2015.

Figure 5.2
SOUTHCOM Theater Security Cooperation Development Process

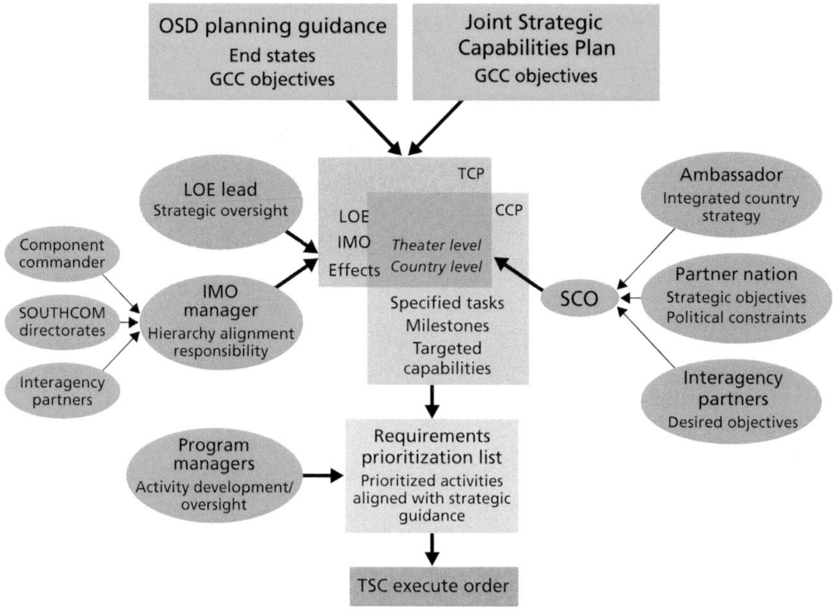

SOURCE: Authors' discussions with SOUTHCOM officials.
NOTES: GCC = Global Combatant Command.
RAND *RR1430-5.2*

the proposed objectives and add desired specified tasks, milestones, and targeted capabilities for achieving higher-level objectives. After the SCOs review the hierarchy of objectives, the draft TCP is reviewed and validated by the IMO managers for alignment with their respective IMOs.[4]

Table 5.1 provides a notional illustration of the nested hierarchical linkages. This process departs from previous TCP development cycles by pushing responsibility for development of more specific objectives closer to activity executors. One IMO manager saw this as a positive change, in that the goal was not to lose specificity or control of the

---

[4] Interview with SOUTHCOM officials, April 2, 2015.

Table 5.1
Notional Illustration of Nesting Objectives

LOE	IMO	Effect	Specified Task	Milestone	Targeted Capability
1. Defense institution building (DIB)	1.1.Ministries of Defense (MODs) capable of planning, coordinating, and conducting DIB activities	1.1.A. Country X MOD planning staff independently generate, plan, and execute DIB activities	1.1.A.1. United States supports MOD with DIB planning education and training	1.1.A.1.A. Staff planning workshop, FY 2016	MOD staff personnel conduct planning exercises with United States
			1.1.A.2. Key leader engagement with MOD to strengthen U.S. support to MOD	1.1.A.2.A. Partner nation developed and led exercise to test staff planning capabilities, FY 2016	MOD seeks U.S. support in developing staff planning capability
		1.1.B. Country X coordinates with interagency and nongovernmental organizations (NGOs) to facilitate DIB development activities	1.1.B.1. Country X military possess capability to integrate interagency and NGO in planning processes	1.1.B.1.A. Country X MOD promotes legislation for appropriate authorities, FY 2017	Chief, Armed Forces, develops interagency and NGO directorate with appropriate resourcing and authorities
				1.1.B.1.B. Chief, Armed Forces, reorganizes directorates to include new interagency and NGO directorate, FY 2018	

SOURCE: RAND analysis.

process but "to switch ownership" to the SCOs working at the country level.[5]

Many respondents noted that, throughout the review process, multiple stakeholder inputs are incorporated into the draft TCP to ensure that SOUTHCOM's programmed activities and programs in development are linked directly to OSD strategic guidance and CCMD IMOs.[6] This occurs early in the process, as described above, with periodic consultations as TCP development progresses. IMO managers provide a strategic-level review to ensure linkages between guidance and programs, while SCOs are responsible for the country-level vetting of programs to ensure alignment with the U.S. embassy's priorities, through its Integrated Country Strategy, in accordance with Presidential Policy Directive 23.[7] In some cases, the SCO will vet proposed objectives against the partner nation's published strategies and priorities to ensure adequate ability on the part of the partner nation to absorb the proposed security cooperation capability.[8]

However, it appears that the IMO managers will in some cases defer to stakeholder inputs in the initial drafting process, resulting in a disconnect between SOUTHCOM guidance and the "realities" at the country level. In one instance, the TCP lacked objectives to cover activities the SCO was already conducting and considered essential to the relationship with the partner nation. One SCO stated that he executed 25 activities in the previous year that were not linked to objectives in the draft TCP.[9] In other scenarios, stakeholders may populate this document with objectives that serve their parochial interests and do not reflect the priorities of the country team—but are now the responsibility of the SCO to synchronize, deconflict, and resource.[10]

---

[5] Interview with SOUTHCOM officials, September 30, 2015.

[6] Interview with SOUTHCOM officials, April 2, 2015.

[7] The White House, "Fact Sheet: U. S. Security Sector Assistance Policy," Presidential Policy Directive 23, April 5, 2013.

[8] Interview with SCO, May 14, 2015.

[9] Interview with SCO, May 14, 2015.

[10] Interview with SCO, May 13, 2015.

SOUTHCOM staff argued that SCO inputs are taken seriously and have considerable impact on the TCP review process, especially with regard to the SCO's ability to effectively manage the span of objective and concomitant activities with limited resources and personnel at the embassy.[11]

SOUTHCOM's Iterative TCP and CCP Development Process Promotes Coordination Between Planners and SCOs

Under the purview of SOUTHCOM's J54 (Security Cooperation Division), CCPs are developed concurrently with the TCP; CCPs use the LOEs, IMOs, and effects from the TCP and then add specified tasks, milestones, and targeted capabilities. The J54 office first submits the draft CCPs to the SCOs, who are responsible for building targeted partner capabilities and milestones in conjunction with the embassy's country team, comprising representatives from Departments of State and Justice, the U.S. Agency for International Development, the FBI, and other government agencies, to better synchronize interagency activities to promote a more comprehensive body of country-level objectives in accordance with Presidential Policy Directive 23.[12] In developing the draft CCP, SCOs work with SOUTHCOM planners during a series of workshops to recommend modifications to the TCP, including IMOs and effects, which in turn affect further refinement of the specified tasks, milestones, and targeted capabilities. The iterative nature of objective development better aligns country-level execution with desired guidance. For example, one SCO stated that he recommended, and SOUTHCOM accepted, the addition of two IMOs and effects in order to align with specified tasks and concomitant programs that the SCO was already executing.[13]

The draft CCP is then submitted to the IMO managers for review to ensure that all proposed CCPs are aligned with their respective IMOs and to make any changes based on the IMO manager's internal AME processes. The draft CCP then returns to the SCO, to receive

[11] Interview with SOUTHCOM officials, May 19, 2015.

[12] Interview with SOUTHCOM officials, April 2, 2015.

[13] Interview with SCO, May 14, 2015.

the ambassador's approval and to confirm that the CCPs are politically viable within the host nation and in alignment with the Department of State's integrated country strategies.[14]

The CCP generally succeeds as an alignment mechanism to ensure a level of coherency among DoD, other interagency organizations operating within a particular country, and the host nation. The CCP development process accounts for the priorities of the interagency and considers host-nation priorities based on SCO engagements and review of host-nation strategic documents.[15] One SOUTHCOM official noted that there was general satisfaction within the SOUTHCOM staff, including the interagency liaisons assigned to the staff, with the level of alignment between DoD and interagency objectives.[16] There was also consensus from officials interviewed that the higher-level guidance, as drawn from the TCP, is considered sufficient for planning at the country level; one SCO interviewed remarked that this guidance, in the form of the hierarchy of objectives, helps him better understand how SOUTHCOM views his country and its relationship to the region, and provides a framework for prioritizing and resourcing activities at the country level.[17] However, as one SCO noted, based on the TCP's annual review cycle, the CCP is too static to provide sufficient guidance to account for more frequently occurring contingencies that were not initially considered in the planning process.[18] For example, in September 2014, unexpected progress in the peace process between the government of Colombia and the representatives of the Revolutionary Armed Forces of Colombia resulted in the SCO prioritizing disarmament, demobilization, and reintegration efforts, where previously they had not been a consideration; consequently, these efforts were not included in or aligned with the TCP.

---

[14] Interview with SOUTHCOM official, May 19, 2015.

[15] Interview with SCO, May 14, 2015.

[16] Interview with SOUTHCOM officials, April 2, 2015.

[17] Interview with SCO, May 14, 2015.

[18] Interview with SCO, May 14, 2015.

SOUTHCOM's Approach to Resourcing and Prioritization of Activities Promotes Synchronization

Once the TCPs and CCPs are published, each security cooperation program manager begins to load the Theater Security Cooperation Management Information System (TSCMIS) with proposed activities, including each activity's alignment with the hierarchy of objectives.[19] This process generally proceeds from January to April and includes several functional planning meetings to review and assess proposed activities, after which each IMO manager will validate activities under the purview of their respective IMO[20] to synchronize activities within each country.[21] SCOs also vet proposed activities, with a focus on the required resources for managing execution of activities within the country. One SOUTHCOM official commented that SCOs "set the throttles" within the host nation, as they have the best perspective on the country's absorptive capability for proposed activities.[22]

Convening a security cooperation ("Horseblanket") conference in June, SOUTHCOM brings together representatives from every program to amalgamate all proposed and validated activities across LOEs and regions to produce a final prioritized list, which is reviewed by a resource board to allocate resources. The Theater Security Cooperation Execute Order is then published to provide final authority to execute each program, generally around August. The execute order is the culmination of the TCP process. It ensures that the SOUTHCOM commander has broad oversight over all activities conducted within the region, and it attempts to synchronize efforts among DoD entities, as well as those of interagency and host-nation organizations.

---

[19] SOUTHCOM has not transitioned to G-TSCMIS because the system lacks capabilities used during the TCP review process. It expects to transition to G-TSCMIS once a new version is released that incorporates SOUTHCOM's data requirements in the FY 2017 activity build cycle. Email exchange, SOUTHCOM official, May 20, 2015.

[20] Interview with SOUTHCOM officials, April 2, 2015.

[21] Interview with SOUTHCOM official, May 19, 2015.

[22] Interview with SOUTHCOM officials, May 21, 2015.

SOUTHCOM Faces Notable Disconnects in Its Multilayered AME Process

In previous years, evaluation of the TCP had been more centralized, but due to forced reductions in staff manning, which reduced the number of personnel in its strategic analysis branch from ten to three, SOUTHCOM transitioned to a decentralized process. Whereas the earlier TCP evaluation was a more comprehensive and robust look at measures of effectiveness or performance, developed as part of the activity build process, the current process is disaggregated, delegating activity evaluation to IMO managers, while J85 (Acquisition Support Division) retains responsibility for strategic-level evaluation. Also driving the transition of the AME program, as one SOUTHCOM official noted, was the perceived non-utility of the earlier AME process, due mainly to its focus on quantitative over qualitative evaluations.[23]

As of spring 2015, SOUTHCOM's new system consisted of several layers of AME conducted independently and specifically geared toward the requirements of each organization. SCOs retained an internal assessment process within the U.S. embassy's country team that regularly, but subjectively, evaluated execution of the previous year's activities and developed a baseline country assessment, both of which drove development of objectives for input to the TCPs and CCPs. For the most part, SOUTHCOM staff did not have any oversight of this assessment capability, with one SCO noting that it was left up to the SCOs to identify what is important and to prioritize inputs into the draft versions of these planning documents.[24]

IMO managers were tasked with developing and executing higher-level internal evaluations of activities executed under their purview (Annex L to USSOUTHCOM Update 1 to FY15–19 TCP [Draft], February 2015) and with supporting J85 in conducting higher-level evaluations—i.e., LOEs or OSD planning guidance end states, as will be related below. However, these lower-level evaluations are not fed directly into the strategic-level AME framework; instead, IMO man-

---

[23] Interview with SOUTHCOM official, May 21, 2015.

[24] Interview with SCO, May 14, 2015.

gers use these lower-level evaluations to develop insights and inform the manager's evaluation of achievement of theater-wide objectives. The disaggregation of AME responsibilities mentioned above has resulted in inconsistency in processes and format among the IMO managers. As an example, within the last TCP review cycle, SOUTHCOM's J3 (Operations Directorate), which has oversight for the countering transnational organized crime LOE, conducted its own mission analysis and directed the component commands to do a capability gap analysis for priority countries, while the J7 (Theater Engagement Directorate), which oversees the humanitarian assistance/disaster relief LOE, contracted with an external organization to conduct a separate gap analysis.

The J85 has responsibility over the campaign assessment process, which includes developing a strategic-level evaluation and culminates in a campaign assessment review board. The final results are presented to the SOUTHCOM commander. The qualitative component of the strategic-level evaluation is the Campaign Assessment Survey, which solicits inputs from subject-matter experts across SOUTHCOM to evaluate overall campaign progress and identify risks and opportunities. An empirical analysis of the strategic environment balances the subjective input from the survey with a quantitative analysis of progress toward achievement of campaign objectives by using indicators that measure environmental conditions.[25] LOE leads evaluate progress toward achieving respective LOE end states, and this evaluation is then fed into the campaign assessment process. The LOE leads individually present their findings to the Campaign Assessment Review Board.

As mentioned above, SOUTHCOM's AME process is still in transition from the previously more centralized FY 2014 TCP assessment, which took a more quantitative look at SOUTHCOM's TCP execution. SOUTHCOM's transition plan is deliberate and recognizes that there is a learning curve to achieving a more robust and comprehensive AME system. Guidance provided in the winter/spring 2015 draft TCP directed programmatic evaluations to focus predominantly on capturing activity performance, with the expectation in future itera-

---

[25] Interview with SOUTHCOM official, May 21, 2015.

tions to expand evaluation to include cost, schedule, and risk analysis metrics.

Planning and AME Challenges and Responses

Challenges

As noted above, SOUTHCOM has developed over the past five years a much more centralized planning process in order to produce a streamlined set of resourced activities, synchronized with strategic guidance and deconflicted among DoD and, to a lesser extent, other U.S. government stakeholders in the region. At the same time, SOUTHCOM has transitioned from a more centralized AME process to a disaggregated process in response to headquarters personnel cuts. The merger of these two influences has created several challenges SOUTHCOM must face in executing its TCP development process.

Several respondents noted an issue with the level of specificity in the coalesced hierarchy of objectives. Previously, objectives were broader and provided excessive latitude to subordinate commands to develop and execute activities. SOUTHCOM staff did not have sufficient awareness of these activities to ensure alignment with the SOUTHCOM commander's intent.[26] Accordingly, SOUTHCOM sought to build a system to capture all security cooperation activities so that the commander "now knows at a particular time of the year what is going on in the [region]."[27] However, some respondents noted that the system has become too specific and inflexible to be useful.[28] This can lead to guidance from component commands or SOUTHCOM directorates that may not reflect current embassy activities or priorities and can complicate the planning process for the security cooperation organization (formerly called the military group) to prioritize and manage resources and personnel to address activities.

---

26 Interview with SOUTHCOM officials, April 2, 2015.

27 Interview with SOUTHCOM official, May 19, 2015.

28 Interview with SOUTHCOM official, September 30, 2015; interview with SCO, May 13, 2015.

Inputs from component commands, which make up a majority of SOUTHCOM's activity execution, are driven by the service's budgeting and resourcing process, which spans a five-year horizon; the TCP review process, on the other hand, is annual. Consequently, SOUTHCOM must overcome the inertia of component-resourced activities to align activity execution to strategic guidance; one SOUTHCOM official noted that "activities are going to happen anyway, regardless of the assessment [or guidance]."[29]

There were mixed opinions regarding the fidelity of TCP objectives to the realities of the SCOs' working environment. While SOUTHCOM staff officials and one SCO interviewed noted an improvement in incorporating SCO recommendations into the TCP, another SCO felt that there was little leverage in shaping SOUTHCOM country-level objectives to the realities of the security cooperation environment within the host nation.[30] It remains to be seen whether the 2015 process changes will alleviate the above concerns.

One official raised an interesting issue regarding SOUTHCOM's ability to comprehensively plan its activities within the interagency environment. Whereas DoD has a very structured and layered approach to strategic planning, typically breaking down objectives into strategic, operational, and tactical levels, other agencies involved in achieving regional end states do not have such a structured approach. As such, aligning objectives at the appropriate strategic level to those of the other agencies presents a challenge to planners. The official noted that "if you talk to the [other interagency organizations], they have [Washington] D.C. and they have implementers, and there is nothing in between."[31] This disconnect between DoD and interagency partners could lead to capability gaps and too much or too little effort expended on plans to achieve regional end states.[32]

---

[29] Interview with SOUTHCOM officials, May 21, 2015.

[30] Interview with SCO, May 13, 2015.

[31] Interview with SOUTHCOM officials, May 21, 2015.

[32] Interview with SOUTHCOM officials, May 21, 2015.

One of the key challenges we noted is SOUTHCOM's ability to comprehensively assess achievement of its stated objectives. With the reduction of personnel in the strategic analysis branch and the disaggregation of AME processes, SOUTHCOM has a reduced ability to analyze how well subordinate objectives are advancing higher-level objectives.[33] At the same time, SOUTHCOM has scoped its TCP objectives based on available resources[34] to make them more realistic, in a shift away from the previously broad and aspirational goals.[35] The combination of these two influences can result in capability gaps—recognized or not—precluding the full achievement of strategic guidance.

The disaggregation of the AME process also presents several challenges to SOUTHCOM. With no centralized and structured process to develop and measure indicators, each IMO manager has the authority to develop an internal process, which results in inconsistency across IMO evaluations.[36] Without strategic analysis branch involvement in IMO/AME processes, security cooperation planners end up evaluating the effectiveness of their own programs, which eliminates the objectivity of the results and thus limits the efficacy of the evaluation. The variation in IMO evaluation appears due in part to the nature of the LOEs to which the IMOs belong. IMOs related to the counterterrorism or countering transnational organized crime LOEs, for example, involve objectives that are relatively more tangible that those of defense institution building. Therefore, the former two LOEs tended toward evaluations with greater fidelity than those of defense institution building, which must address the challenges inherent in measuring progress of defense institutions.[37] One respondent felt that, while this discrepancy exists regarding the quality of evaluation among LOEs, it had not negatively affected decisions of prioritization or resourcing of pro-

---

[33] Interview with SOUTHCOM officials, May 21, 2015.

[34] Interview with SOUTHCOM officials, April 2, 2015.

[35] Interview with SOUTHCOM officials, May 21, 2015.

[36] Interview with SOUTHCOM officials, May 21, 2015.

[37] Interview with SOUTHCOM officials, September 30, 2015.

grammed activities.[38] Exacerbating this issue of variation in evaluation, as one respondent noted, is a lack of motivation on the part of some or simply the lack of individuals assigned to an IMO to conduct high-fidelity evaluations, based on insufficient resources or time and combined with the fact that activity level evaluation remains internal to the IMO manager and is not incorporated into SOUTHCOM's campaign analysis.[39]

As noted earlier, SOUTHCOM AME guidance limits evaluation of activities to performance metrics only, while noting that future refinement of the AME process will include other aspects, such as cost, schedule, risk analysis, and program adequacy and effectiveness in support of operational objectives. Thus, strategic guidance from SOUTHCOM does not necessarily reflect the realities within the host nations, with one respondent noting that SCOs "are not enamored" with SOUTHCOM because of this misalignment between the guidance promulgated and what the country requires.[40] Another respondent remarked that there is a "weak" connection between the SCO level and the formal strategic assessments presented to the commander.[41]

SOUTHCOM Has Responded to These Challenges in Several Ways

Many of the challenges noted above have been recognized by SOUTHCOM staff, who are working to institute corrective measures. To address the disconnect between the country teams and SOUTHCOM staff, the J55 (Strategic Planning Division), which has responsibility for TCP development, conducts a regional trip to visit with SCOs in April to receive direct input regarding the viability of the objectives and better align guidance with country-level "reality." Additionally, several SOUTHCOM officials acknowledged this disconnect and the need to balance SOUTHCOM requirements with SCO workload and limited resources through iterative discussion between SOUTH-

---

[38] Interview with SOUTHCOM official, September 30, 2015.

[39] Interview with SOUTHCOM official, September 30, 2015; interview with SOUTHCOM officials, May 21, 2015.

[40] Interview with SOUTHCOM official, May 19, 2015.

[41] Interview with SOUTHCOM officials, May 21, 2015.

COM staffers and SCOs.[42] This has already had a positive effect, with one SCO noting that SOUTHCOM headquarters was more receptive in the previous year than in years prior to incorporating SCO inputs, and consequently there was general agreement in the embassy that the TCP and CCP were more closely aligned with host-nation requirements.[43] Regarding the fidelity of the campaign assessment to the actual achievement of strategic objectives, many SOUTHCOM officials acknowledge that there are gaps in SOUTHCOM's ability to comprehensively assess the TCP, and, as mentioned earlier, the current AME process already indicates that future evaluations will expand their scope to include more effective measurements for determining achievement of strategic guidance. An earlier RAND study that addressed effectiveness and efficiency of security cooperation mechanisms may prove useful to SOUTHCOM as it seeks to improve its AME process.[44] With SOUTHCOM staff already working on the FY 2017 TCP, efforts are under way to collect inputs from all stakeholders on how to improve the balance between specific guidance and latitude in activity execution.[45]

RAND Evaluation and Revision of Selected Partner-Nation Objectives

Using the SMART framework developed for this study, we conducted an initial evaluation of the country-level security cooperation objectives provided by OSD. After conducting interviews with SOUTHCOM officials, we determined that these objectives were derived from TCP effects but lacked the additional detail provided by specified tasks, milestones, and targeted capabilities. In the following section, we detail

---

[42] Interview with SOUTHCOM official, May 19, 2015.

[43] Interview with SCO, May 14, 2015.

[44] Jennifer D. P. Moroney, David E. Thaler, and Joe Hogler, *Review of Security Cooperation Mechanisms Combatant Commands Utilize to Build Partner Capacity*, Santa Monica, Calif.: RAND Corporation, RR-413-OSD, 2013.

[45] Interview with SOUTHCOM officials, April 2, 2015.

the initial trends we identified in the evaluation of these effects-level security cooperation objectives; in the subsequent section, we provide our summary evaluation of the full hierarchy of security cooperation objectives found in the TCP. As the following summaries will show, the limited scope of the OSD-provided objectives significantly limited their SMARTness and would not be particularly valuable for supporting decisions at the policymaking level.

Initial SMART Evaluation

Table 5.2 summarizes the trends we found in our initial analysis of the OSD-provided objectives for countries in SOUTHCOM's area of responsibility. As noted above, the OSD-provided objectives we assessed were based on only one of the six levels in SOUTHCOM's nesting model, resulting in generally poor evaluations in the specific, measurable, and relevant/results-oriented categories. Due to limited documentation of SOUTHCOM's particular security cooperation environment, evaluation of achievability proved difficult. Almost all objectives included a desired end date, but the relationship among level of effort, resources, and the objective deadline was unclear.

SOUTHCOM's Multilevel Hierarchy of Objectives Demonstrated SMART Characteristics

In the process of developing the synchronization product mentioned earlier, SOUTHCOM addresses many of the issues raised in the RAND team's initial evaluation. While the initial RAND framework was tailored to evaluate individual, country-level objectives, this framework was expanded to evaluate SOUTHCOM's more holistic hierarchy of objectives. The following is a summary of the ways in which SOUTHCOM's overall hierarchy of security cooperation objectives addresses many of the questions posed within the RAND framework.

Specific—Greater Granularity

As one SOUTHCOM official noted, earlier versions of objectives had been fairly broad and allowed for excessive latitude to CCMDs in exe-

Table 5.2
Initial OSD/SOUTHCOM Country Objectives Evaluation

SMART Criterion	Evaluation
Specific	• We evaluated 30% of the objectives as unsatisfactory (red), 0% as satisfactory (green), and the rest as neither satisfactory nor unsatisfactory (yellow). • The primary reason for the unsatisfactory/red rating was a lack of information regarding which U.S. entity was responsible for objective achievement or where within a partner nation the objective was focused.
Measurable	• We evaluated 60% of the objectives as unsatisfactory (red), 30% as satisfactory (green), and the rest as neither satisfactory nor unsatisfactory (yellow). • Objectives did not clearly stipulate what to measure or how to measure change of the desired end state, nor was there an indication of what constituted a sufficient level of achievement.
Achievable	• An assessment was not possible, due to insufficient information provided to indicate the security environment, political situation, or availability of U.S. forces to determine the achievability of a particular objective (gray).
Relevant and results-oriented	• We evaluated 50% of the objectives as satisfactory (green), while the remaining objectives were evenly split between unsatisfactory (red) and neither satisfactory or unsatisfactory (yellow). • While objectives in this category generally demonstrated alignment and relationships to higher-level guidance, they were mostly formulated as outputs rather than outcomes.
Time-bound	• We evaluated over 50% of objectives as neither satisfactory or unsatisfactory (yellow). Nearly 40% of the remaining objectives were satisfactory (green). • This evaluation is based on two factors: (1) the study team's inability to determine a relationship between time limits for achievement and the resourcing available and (2) the majority of deadlines being five years or greater.

SOURCE: RAND analysis.

cuting activities in alignment with strategic guidance.[46] SOUTHCOM J55 worked to increase the granularity of effects and specified tasks with the expected end result of removing any "gray areas."[47] In the FY 2016/2017 TCP review process, there was a push to generate more-

[46] Interview with SOUTHCOM officials, April 2, 2015.

[47] Interview with SOUTHCOM officials, April 2, 2015.

specific objectives with a higher level of granularity, to ensure that all activities conducted in the area of responsibility are recognized and validated by the combatant commander.[48] In striving for specificity, there is a risk that planners will conflate objectives and tasks. In some cases, specificity of objectives was perceived as going too far, with one SCO regarding the objectives as "too in the weeds."[49] That said, objectives require some level of specificity that can then be linked to even more-specific tasks.

The synchronization product includes a column that designates an OPR with oversight for the respective LOE, IMO, and effect; there is also a column that includes all supporting organizations that provide resources for or management of activities associated with the particular objective.

Measurable—Nested Objectives Supported Measurability

As noted above, the objectives initially evaluated by the RAND team were lacking in measurable indicators and concrete methods to determine any level of achievement of a particular objective. SOUTHCOM's hierarchy of objectives, however, link concrete targeted capabilities and milestone events that demonstrated the desired capability with country-level specified tasks and effects. This nested approach provides a pathway for clearly measuring achievement of security cooperation objectives. For example, SOUTHCOM's TCP includes a specified task directing engagement with counterterrorism forces from certain countries to promote interoperability. While this particular specified task is difficult to measure, the subordinate targeted capabilities provide the additional detail needed to measure achievement of this task.

Achievable—TCP Development Process Promoted Analysis of Achievability

While SOUTHCOM's TCP does not directly address many of the concerns noted in the RAND framework regarding achievability, the TCP development process contributes to the achievability of each objective.

---

[48] Interview with SOUTHCOM officials, April 2, 2015.

[49] Interview with SCO, May 13, 2015.

During the various levels of review, the hierarchy of objectives is vetted not only against DoD strategic guidance but also against other U.S. agency and even partner-nation priorities and requirements.[50] Specified tasks, targeted capabilities, and milestone events, as well as the programs resourced to them, as part of the CCP, must be validated by the Chief of Mission to ensure effective prioritization and resourcing of activities at the conclusion of SOUTHCOM's annual security cooperation ("Horseblanket") conference. In this sense, the objectives alone do not necessarily account for their assessed achievability, but the overall process does appear to account for this criterion by design.

Relevant and Results-Oriented

Similar to the initial RAND evaluation, the current system clearly demonstrates linkages throughout the objective hierarchy.

Time-Bound

Again, similar to the initial RAND evaluation, the current system clearly establishes timelines for the achievement of the security cooperation objectives. Timelines were less than five years in length and required the documentation of particular milestones to achieve during each annual period to ensure that progress is made toward achieving higher-level guidance.

Conclusion

SOUTHCOM has developed a structured process for the development of its TCP and CCPs. Its Phase Zero Nesting Model provides a framework to clearly demonstrate linkages between country-level activities and strategic-level guidance, while minimizing guidance ambiguity. The TCP and CCP process is robust and provides several mechanisms for ensuring alignment to interagency organizations, including U.S. embassy approval of CCPs. The process is iterative and collaborative to compensate for the potential inertia of security cooperation programs developed on the five-year budget planning cycle by the military ser-

---

[50] Interview with security cooperation official, May 14, 2015.

vices. SOUTHCOM has, thus, worked to develop SMART objectives, as well as a SMART security cooperation planning system. By designating responsible stakeholders, measurable indicators, and manageable timelines, among other concerns raised in the RAND framework, the system provides a practical means of translating SOUTHCOM's theater end states into operational activities, while ensuring that the SOUTHCOM commander has significant oversight over all security cooperation activities conducted within the region. Given the 2015 change in the nesting model to remove specified tasks, milestones, and targeted capabilities from SOUTHCOM's TCP, there is a risk that details important to ensuring SMARTness at the CCMD level will be lost. However, if security cooperation planners manage the linkages between the TCP and CCPs well, this risk should be mitigated. With implementation of formal mechanisms to ensure that SCO input is reconciled with stakeholder inputs, SOUTHCOM's architecture for nesting hierarchical objectives could potentially serve as a model for other CCMDs.

SOUTHCOM lacks a rigorous and in-depth capability to provide feedback regarding country-level activities and their contribution to achieving higher-level objectives. Due mainly to the significant reductions in personnel within the J8 (Resources and Assessments Directorate), the lack of a centralized AME process has led planners to devise individualized ad hoc systems that are not easily integrated for review at higher levels. Moreover, when managers are also responsible for evaluating execution of their own programs, there is the potential for overly positive evaluations. This creates serious problems in providing planners with an objective assessment to refine and improve the commander's guidance.

SOUTHCOM officials realize they are in a transition period, and they are making incremental progress toward a more comprehensive AME program. The foundations for an effective evaluation system are already in place: The TCP development process is already well accepted within SOUTHCOM, and the Phase Zero Nesting Model is a tool that provides the ability to clearly disseminate strategic-level guidance down to the country level. A SMART system must facilitate development of effective security cooperation objectives within the context of an effective AME program. Although SOUTHCOM may have regressed in terms of AME, it has a relatively strong structure for establishing objectives.

CHAPTER SIX

Findings and Recommendations

By most accounts, security cooperation planning and coordination has improved tremendously over the past 15 years. Guidance has become more detailed regarding goals and expectations. Planning is robust and involves many stakeholders. Coordination is facilitated through formal and informal communication, including focused workshops. Nevertheless, CCMDs continue to face significant challenges developing security cooperation objectives with sufficient detail to allow systematic, meaningful evaluations of progress.

Chapters One and Two included some insights on these challenges, while Chapters Three through Five focused on challenges and best practices at PACOM, EUCOM, and SOUTHCOM, respectively. In this chapter, we highlight six findings and recommendations for improvements that we believe are particularly important for all those involved in security cooperation.

Effective objectives form the foundations for effective AME and, more generally, an effective security cooperation planning system. This system should allow stakeholders to understand more clearly the extent to which security cooperation efforts are having the desired effects. We hope that addressing the findings and recommendations in Table 6.1 will help partner-nation officials, U.S. planners and program implementers, and OSD, State Department, and congressional overseers to better understand their common objectives, and thus help these officials strengthen effective activities and redirect or abandon ineffective ones.

Table 6.1
Analyses of CCMD Planning and AME Country Objectives

General Finding	Recommendation
1. Most individual country objectives were not SMART.	1. OSD should provide SMART criteria and prioritization guidance to CCMDs and evaluate their performance accordingly.
2. CCMD security cooperation planning was SMARTer than individual country objectives.	2. OSD and the Joint Staff should work with CCMDs to create a SMART security cooperation planning system centered on country plans. Creating SMART country objectives is not enough.
3. CCMD security cooperation planning could benefit from greater standardization.	3. OSD and the Joint Staff should work with CCMDs to establish a common theater planning hierarchy for security cooperation objectives, with standard terminology and a standard SMART-objective review process.
4. Responsibility and priority for developing country objectives differed by CCMD.	4. CCMDs should integrate security cooperation elements of planning under a single authority.
5. Understanding of the SMART concept varied among stakeholders.	5. DoD should incorporate the SMART concept more formally into security cooperation training.
6. SMART objectives did not adequately serve as a foundation for security cooperation AME.	6. OSD should establish a security cooperation framework that links SMART objectives to AME processes and requirements at the strategic and country levels.

Finding 1: Most Individual Country Objectives Were Not SMART

Although there were planners at each CCMD working to improve security cooperation objectives, most objectives were not yet SMART, especially in terms of being measurable, achievable, or time-bound. Three reasons stood out. First, efforts to systematically improve objective design are relatively new and require time to be understood by the many stakeholders involved. Second, these efforts depend largely on the knowledge and determination of individual CCMD planners working within larger, more complex planning structures. Third, staff do not have an effective process for passing along priorities to their successors and maintaining momentum in the face of frequent job rotations. CCMDs generally found RAND's SMART evaluation worksheet useful, and we believe it could institutionalize and standardize what are currently somewhat nascent and ad hoc efforts. CCMD staff may be able to help refine the framework. The "relevant and results-oriented" criterion, in particular, may need revisions to account for the "cookie-cutter" phenomenon that exists to some degree in all the CCMDs we examined. This involves the nearly verbatim repetition of objective language from the strategic to the country level, which may ensure that objectives are aligned with higher-level guidance but not necessarily guarantee they are in accord with the requirements of particular partners.

For most objectives, achievability could not be determined because risk factors, such as availability of resources and potential partner actions, were not documented. The difficulties inherent in predicting long-term resource availability and partner actions probably make achievability the most challenging aspect of designing SMART objectives. Although staff cannot predict future resource levels overall, clearer prioritization of activities, objectives, partners, and resource requests can improve the ability to understand the funding risks activities have relative to each other. Additional OSD guidance about how to prioritize activities, objectives, and partners could help CCMD and SCO staff to prioritize resource requests. Part of this prioritization guidance could also direct CCMD and SCO staff to analyze and document partner willingness and ability to progress in a desired direction. U.S. military foreign area officers, civil affairs specialists, and civilian U.S. embassy staff could also be leveraged to help analyze risks and opportunities related to potential partner actions. Improved guidance and analysis would help OSD set expectations and make more informed decisions, creating a virtuous cycle of communication to inform achievability estimates.

Recommendation 1: OSD Should Provide SMART Criteria and Prioritization Guidance to CCMDs and Evaluate Their Performance Accordingly

The SMART framework we described in Chapter One could serve as the foundation for OSD guidance on developing SMART security cooperation objectives and a potential tool for CCMDs and OSD to evaluate them. OSD may want to work with CCMDs to test the framework for a year and suggest modifications. Additional guidance on (1) prioritizing objectives, partners, and resources and (2) analyzing partner willingness and ability to achieve these objectives could be inserted into several documents, including a DoD instruction on security cooperation, the security cooperation section of OSD planning guidance, and in each CCMD TCP.

Finding 2: CCMD Security Cooperation Planning Was SMARTer Than Individual Country Objectives

Although we found that most country plan objectives failed the SMART test, our analysis of country plans overall and other supporting documents showed more-positive results. For example, SOUTHCOM's plans facilitated SMARTness by creating OPRs, capability milestones, and metrics for evaluating impact. PACOM used "partner capability roadmaps" to complement its country plans. PACOM's CSCPs and capability development working groups also supported a SMARTer security cooperation planning system. EUCOM's annual conferences, SAS Plan scoping statements, and CCP roadmaps were all designed to help create a SMART system and compensate for weaknesses in individual country objectives. All CCMDs also incorporated interests of other relevant stakeholders into their planning to varying degrees.

Recommendation 2: OSD and the Joint Staff Should Work with CCMDs to Create a SMART Security Cooperation Planning System Centered on Country Plans; Creating SMART Country Objectives Is Not Enough

SMART country objectives cannot be effective, and may not even be possible, without a planning system that does two things. First, a SMART system should link country objectives to higher-level strategies and lower-level tasks. Country objectives help translate strategic guidance into tasks, and they put individual tasks in the context of U.S. foreign policy and national security goals. Second, a SMART system should support security cooperation AME. Assessments of partner capabilities and will, monitoring of programs, and evaluations of impact allow planners to design and revise objectives over time.[1] AME also helps stakeholders to prioritize objectives and allocate resources. The CCMDs have elements of such a system, but they are not organized around a SMART framework. RAND's proposed framework can be applied not only to country objectives but to country plans and to the other planning components described in Chapters Three through Five. OSD and the Joint Staff could work with CCMDs—through guidance, workshops, and improved training—to incorporate a SMART approach that nests SMART country objectives within SMART country plans within a SMART security cooperation planning process that incorporates inputs from security cooperation stakeholders beyond CCMD staff, as well as a robust AME infrastructure. (See the appendix or an illustrative template of a SMART country plan.)

[1] Such an approach could also take into greater account the suggestion for a more risk-based analysis of security cooperation objectives, as was made by a EUCOM official cited in Chapter Four.

Finding 3: CCMD Security Cooperation Planning Could Benefit from Greater Standardization

Although CCMD security cooperation planning included many components of a SMART system, the ways in which plans were designed varied extensively. What their plans and processes all shared, however, was complexity. For an analyst looking across CCMDs, in fact, the unit of analysis for SMART evaluations—i.e., which set of objectives to start with—was sometimes difficult to identify. CCMDs have different objective hierarchies, and they do not define their terms in the same way. For example, PACOM focused on objectives within CSCPs and CCPs, which were linked but not in a hierarchical way. SOUTHCOM, on the other hand, nested objectives for desired partner capabilities firmly within a series of higher-level objectives, leading ultimately to OSD planning guidance end states.

Terminology also varied considerably. For example, EUCOM used scoping statements rather than country objectives. It was not clear whether EUCOM's outcomes were comparable to PACOM's effects. PACOM had a range of "objective-like" planning elements, including IMOs, effects, measures, indicators, country end states, country objectives, and partner capabilities. SOUTHCOM had LOEs, IMOs, effects, specified tasks, milestones, and targeted capabilities, which were nested from broader to more specific.

For stakeholders both within and outside the CCMDs, there could be significant benefits if the process of developing a security cooperation planning structure—and a country plan structure in particular—were standardized. For example, the benefits of using the same terminology would facilitate a common understanding within the CCMDs and among policymakers in DoD and other departments. AME would be simplified because terms, plan design, and coordination processes would be more consistent. Transparency would improve for policymakers and congressional overseers.

Recommendation 3: OSD and the Joint Staff Should Work with CCMDs to Establish a Common Theater Planning Hierarchy for Security Cooperation Objectives, with Standard Terminology and a Standard SMART-Objective Review Process

Because CCMD staffs have invested countless hours refining, documenting, and utilizing their planning structures, as well as familiarizing their leaders with these structures, they are not easily changed. We recommend one of two approaches, described below, to improving standardization. Both involve OSD and the Joint Staff convening a series of workshops and documenting results in a DoD security cooperation planning handbook. Both approaches would also include the creation of a standardized review process—led by either OSD or the CCMDs—that ensures stakeholders have a shared view of DoD's objectives on a country-by-country basis.

The first approach would focus on designing a model planning hierarchy for security cooperation, documenting this model in a handbook, and then tasking CCMDs to transition to the model over a two-year period. This transition time would allow for ongoing planning, programming, and budgeting processes to reach the end of their budget cycle. With this approach, we recommend building the model primarily from the existing hierarchy of one CCMD, rather than picking various components from all CCMDs or trying to create a new hierarchy from scratch. Picking various components could result in a Frankenstein monster hybrid, in which the components cannot function effectively together because they were not designed to work together. The disruptive effort required to create a new hierarchy would only be worthwhile if existing systems were all deeply flawed, which is not the case, according to our analysis. The problems are less about each individual CCMD system but rather the difficulties in understanding and utilizing the systems beyond the CCMD itself, so that they support the needs of OSD, the Joint Staff, the State Department, and other officials. Given that each CCMD system already has SMART components that have been tested in real-world conditions, it would not make sense to start from scratch. We recommend using SOUTHCOM's hierarchy as the starting point, because we found it to be the least complex and best integrated. Designing a model hierarchy might prove more challenging but would likely result in greater standardization and thus make security cooperation planning more useful for stakeholders beyond the CCMDs.

The second approach would forgo creating a model hierarchy and instead focus first on developing a common terminology and then on a gradual alignment of hierarchies that is documented in a security cooperation planning handbook. In this approach, OSD and the Joint Staff would work with CCMDs to agree to terms for the various levels of security cooperation–related objectives, plans, and processes within each CCMD's larger planning system. The handbook would not only define these terms but also describe how they fit within a SMART security cooperation planning system. In a second round of workshops, OSD and the Joint Staff would lead structured discussions focused on documenting how CCMD systems align when reviewed together. Planning structures could differ, but their differences would be described and justified within the DoD handbook. This approach might allow CCMDs greater flexibility to tailor their approaches but could be more challenging for stakeholders outside the CCMDs to understand.

Finding 4: Responsibility and Priority for Developing Country Objectives Differed by CCMD

Each of the three CCMDs we examined had a process for developing and reviewing country-level objectives. However, in addition to defining these objectives differently, CCMDs prioritized the formulation of country objectives differently and assigned the primary responsibility for this task to personnel in different positions. Having placed much of its planning energies into IMO development, PACOM focused relatively little attention on creating country objectives. In the past, country desk officers within the J5 were assigned responsibility for developing country end states and objectives according to a basic template that reflected higher-level IMOs, without much input from SCOs or service components. At the time of our research, country objectives did not appear to play a significant role in security cooperation planning and implementation.

EUCOM had a process for developing "scoping statements" that customized standardized LOAs to the situations of particular partner nations. These narrative statements were drafted by functional OPRs on the CCMD staff or relevant service component and reviewed by SCO/SDOs and CCMD desk officers.

In contrast to PACOM and to a lesser extent EUCOM, SOUTHCOM took a holistic approach to planning and objective development. In this command, relatively senior officials were responsible for integrating all the elements of LOEs, from theater-level IMOs to country-level effects, tasks, and milestones, which involved gathering input from other members of the CCMD staff, the service components, and the SCOs. This integrative approach helped ensure that planning elements were both hierarchically nested and appropriately particularized. This helped to resolve any tensions between guidance from higher headquarters and emerging opportunities on the ground.

Recommendation 4: CCMDs Should Integrate Security Cooperation Elements of Planning Under a Single Authority

Although CCMDs must be able to organize themselves, SOUTHCOM's example of integration managers responsible for theater- to country-level LOE planning shows how SMARTness can be more easily injected into the system if a small set of qualified and empowered individuals are placed in charge of managing most elements of the planning hierarchy with input from important stakeholders. Of course, SOUTHCOM is a relatively small, security cooperation–focused CCMD. Creating an integrated theater and country planning process for security cooperation is more difficult in larger and more functionally diverse CCMDs. However, both PACOM and EUCOM have already taken steps in this direction, the former by establishing an LOE focused on security cooperation and the latter by establishing a process for customizing country-level LOAs. But more work is needed in these CCMDs to reduce organizational and procedural barriers between theater and country security cooperation planning and objective development.

Finding 5: Understanding of the SMART Concept Varied Among Stakeholders

Many OSD and CCMD staff directly responsible for integrating security cooperation efforts demonstrated a clear understanding for the importance of well-designed, detailed security cooperation objectives. Some even promoted use of the SMART concept among others involved in the process of designing or implementing security cooperation objectives. For example, EUCOM security cooperation managers emphasized the value of a SMART approach to U.S. embassy country team members developing security cooperation scoping statements. For the most part, however, communication of the SMART concept across DoD was informal and ad hoc. Security cooperation managers, while knowledgeable themselves, did not have the time to personally educate stakeholders across their commands, at service component commands, and at embassies, nor did they have time to thoroughly revise every relevant objective coming in from these locations.

Recommendation 5: DoD Should Incorporate the SMART Concept More Formally into Security Cooperation Training

We recommend that OSD develop a training briefing, based on RAND's SMART framework and briefings and papers that OSD and the CCMD staffs have already developed. OSD could then work with the Defense Institute of Security Assistance Management, CCMDs, and others to integrate SMART objective development into their curricula.

Additionally, we recommend revising the OSD TCP planners handbook to incorporate these recommendations. Coordinating these revisions will support socialization of the recommendations among the CCMDs and other stakeholders to ensure that a careful balance between CCMD planning requirements and OSD standardization guidance is struck.

Finding 6: SMART Objectives Did Not Adequately Serve as a Foundation for Security Cooperation Assessment, Monitoring, and Evaluation

While each of the three CCMDs we reviewed supplied examples of good planning and AME practices, none had a fully integrated system for developing SMART objectives through assessments at the theater and country levels, followed by regular monitoring and periodic evaluation of these objectives. PACOM had a well-developed, albeit complex, LOE evaluation framework, based on mostly regional IMOs. However, it lacked a systematic process for monitoring and evaluating the implementation of country plans. The establishment of such a process was hampered by the dearth of SMART country objectives linking IMOs to security cooperation activities. PACOM's capability development roadmaps could provide the basis for country-level monitoring and evaluation, but besides formulating better objectives, this would require specifying roles, responsibilities, and timelines for metrics development, as well as data collection, processing, and analysis.

LOA progress reports were the basis for AME at EUCOM. Representing a largely subjective review of progress toward LOA scoping goals, the reports' results were integrated into country and thematic assessments by the command's assessment division. For various reasons (e.g., lack of experience, time, access to relevant information), EUCOM's scoping statement was often not well written, and, as a consequence, progress reports varied in quality.

As mentioned above, SOUTHCOM had an integrated, comprehensive security cooperation planning process that resulted in SMART objectives at the theater and country levels. However, its AME process was decentralized and ad hoc, in part because of budget cutbacks that disproportionately affected assessment personnel. AME results were not easily integrated and—because implementers evaluated their own efforts—lacked objectivity. But given SOUTHCOM's existing planning framework, we believe this situation could be remedied with consistent guidance and somewhat greater resources devoted to AME.

Recommendation 6: OSD Should Establish a Security Cooperation Framework That Links SMART Objectives to AME Processes and Requirements at the Strategic and Country Levels

Our analysis of security cooperation planning and assessment has shown that objective development and AME processes in the three CCMDs we examined are inconsistent in their application and quality, both within and across commands. While there will always be some differences in how each CCMD plans, greater standardization in terms of organizing, defining, and appraising the elements of theater and country plans should improve the quality and consistency of objective development and AME. Such elements would include lines of IMOs and country objectives, as well as the metrics used to assess, monitor, and evaluate their status, progress, impediments, and achievements, such as measures of performance, effectiveness, and impact.

Ideally, OSD would lead this standardization process, with input from planning and assessment experts in the CCMDs, the services, the Defense Security Cooperation Agency, and security cooperation offices. OSD could start with a framework spelling out the basic elements of security cooperation plans and specifying AME roles and responsibilities for metrics development, data collection and analysis, and review and approval. The guidance could also describe the principal AME products and the frequency with which they should be inputted, reported, or distributed, as well as the systems and processes that would be used to ensure that AME activities were synchronized. OSD could then support the framework through additional guidance, participation in workshops, and providing inputs to training.

This also dovetails with the aforementioned desire of staff at EUCOM to have OSD ask *why* security cooperation activities do or do not work in order to focus CCMD staff on the impact level of evaluation rather than the output level.[2]

Conclusion

In sum, despite advances in theater campaign planning in recent years, DoD does not yet have a sufficiently standardized and integrated approach to security cooperation planning—particularly in such areas as objective development and AME that would enable DoD leaders, the administration, and Congress to gauge the extent to which global security cooperation resources are being appropriately targeted and effectively employed. Furthermore, the lack of SMART objectives, particularly at the country level, is an important reason why it has been difficult to establish a firm connection between the partnering goals expressed in national strategy documents and the actual activities being conducted by, with, and through partner nations. Fortunately, the establishment of an OSD office focused on security cooperation, and the development of innovative planning and AME models in the CCMDs and other stakeholder organizations, means that the time is ripe for the creation of a common DoD security cooperation planning framework with well-defined components and robust, top-to-bottom linkages. Constructing such a framework will require OSD and the Joint Staff, in consultation with other security cooperation stakeholders, to issue guidance on standardized planning hierarchies, terminologies, and SMART objective criteria. Additionally, further integration of the organizations involved in theater and country planning and AME will be needed, as well as improved training of CCMD staff personnel in objectives and metrics development.

---

[2] Interview with EUCOM headquarters officials, in-person interview with author, May 13, 2015.

APPENDIX

SMART Country Planning

SMART objectives are a necessary but insufficient condition to improved security cooperation planning at the country level. This is because one cannot completely fit all of the elements of the SMART construct into the confines of single phrase or even paragraph without transforming an objective into an indecipherable agglomeration. To avoid this outcome, the planner must ensure that SMARTness resides in the plan that describes, justifies, and supports the objective rather than just in the objective itself. Drawing from existing best practices in CCMD country planning, in this appendix we first provide illustrative examples of objectives for a notional partner nation that demonstrate many of the SMART criteria discussed in this report. We then show how objectives might be embedded within a country plan whose SMART elements are interlaced throughout the plan.

Illustrative SMART Objectives

The following are ten notional security cooperation objectives for the fictional country of Bandaria, which are meant to be broadly representative of the LOAs currently carried out by various regional CCMDs:

1. The Bandarian Ministry of Defense establishes a special unit responsible for monitoring and disrupting domestic and international terrorist network fundraising and other financial activities in two years.

2. The Bandarian Ministry of Defense's peacekeeping operations center offers education and training courses to military and civilian officials of regional partner nations in three years.
3. The Bandarian Ministry of Defense supports expanded access to U.S. military forces, including overflight, temporary blanket clearances, and use of air and sea ports, in support of training exercises and peacetime and wartime contingencies within two years.
4. The Bandarian navy develops a joint plan with customs enforcement for detecting and intercepting illicit nuclear-related materials in the country's ports and harbors within one year.
5. Within two years, the Bandarian Ministry of Defense issues a comprehensive report on gaps in its capabilities to support civilian authorities during an all-hazards event—and the resources required to fill these gaps.
6. In five years, the Bandarian navy takes the lead in planning and conducting a series of annual maritime security exercises with partner navies aimed at improving regional capabilities to detect and interdict illicit trafficking in weapons of mass destruction–related materials.
7. In three years, the Bandarian army has established facilities for the safeguarding and disposal of chemical/biological weapons and weapon-related materials and authorized these facilities to be inspected on a biannual basis by UN or U.S. experts.
8. Bandaria conducts a joint naval exercise in two years with regional partner navies and the U.S. Navy to practice procedures for avoiding confrontations between vessels in disputed international waters.
9. In one year, the Bandarian Ministry of Defense and U.S. regional CCMD develop a cyberspace cooperation terms of reference that defines roles and responsibilities, methods of work, business practices, and mission-essential tasks.
10. In two years, the Bandarian air force has the airlift capability and capacity to support a battalion-size regional peacekeeping operation for three months.

In general, the above objectives are SMARTer with respect to some dimensions of our evaluation construct than others. Most obviously, each objective is time-bound in that it indicates the number of years that are expected for its completion, which in every case is five years or less. To a certain extent, each objective also conforms to our definition of specificity. For example, each objective indicates which organization within the partner government—the Ministry of Defense, the navy, the army, or the air force—is responsible for achieving the objective, whether it relates to counterterrorism, peacekeeping, maritime security, etc. That said, the objectives do not indicate which organization within the U.S. military is responsible for helping to ensure their attainment. Nor do the objectives fully address what should be done. For example, which terrorist networks are intended as the focus of the first objective? What education and training courses should be offered by the peacekeeping operations center mentioned in the second objective?

Similarly, measurability is only partly addressed by the above objectives. Most are observable and clear in terms of the unit of measure—e.g., an element of force structure, a facility, an exercise, or a report. But the baseline for measurement is not always specified; for example, the final objective does not state how much airlift capacity the Bandarian air force currently has. Nor is it always apparent how much or many of an action or thing is desired, such as the series of maritime security exercises called for in objective 6. Finally there is no indication of whether a sustainable system is in place to monitor progress in accomplishing the objectives.

Lacking a context for the above objectives, relevance/results-orientation and achievability cannot be easily discerned. One can therefore only speculate about probable U.S. strategic goals or regional security cooperation capabilities, since they are not referenced in the objectives themselves.

Illustrative SMART Country Plan

The following partial country plan (or LOA) for Bandaria illustrates how objectives—in this case objective 10—can meet SMART criteria when augmented by other components of the plan. These components include a partner end state, which is a broader, longer-term, and more aspirational goal than its associated objectives; a strategic/mission analysis that provides the foundation for the end state; and a concept development that spells out more precisely what is intended in terms of objectives, when, by what means, and by whom.

End State

Bandaria has the capability to deploy and the capacity to sustain a regional peacekeeping force that can independently conduct tactical operations for a period of at least one year.

Strategic/Mission Analysis

The bullets below summarize the strategic and mission analysis sections of the country plan that pertain to the achievability and relevance/results-orientation of the intended end state:

- Although Bandaria is relatively stable, two of its neighbors have requested external assistance in the past five years to cope with persistent insecurity stemming from insurgent attacks against civilian populations.
- OSD planning guidance and the TCP emphasize the importance of encouraging Bandaria to play a leading role in regional peacekeeping operations, thus reducing the need for significant U.S. military involvement.
- It is currently estimated that Bandaria can deploy and sustain two companies of peacekeeping forces for approximately one month.
- To deploy and support a force capable of conducting independent tactical operations will require a substantial airlift capability, due to the long distance from major ports to areas of instability and the poor regional ground infrastructure.
- Bandaria's air force is currently overstretched, underfunded, and in desperate need of modernization; in particular, it faces a major challenge in replacing its aging fleet of medium air transport aircraft, only one-third of which are operational and in high demand.

- Although Bandaria's current government is imbued with an anti-Western ideology, its security relationship with Washington has improved markedly in recent years, as demonstrated by its participation in joint military exercises, personnel exchanges, education and training programs, and some military sales.
- A number of Department of State, DoD, and U.S. Air Force venues exist to facilitate discussions between the United States and Bandaria on building the latter's airlift capacity, as well as programs to execute, monitor, and evaluate an agreed-to capacity-building plan; additionally, there are few U.S. government legal or policy barriers to cooperating with Bandaria in the security realm.
- Despite its limited defense acquisition budget, Bandaria has placed a high priority on modernizing its air transport fleet and has begun to explore the possibility of purchasing new aircraft from several major foreign suppliers, including the United States. The Bandarian air force also has a relatively large and professional workforce that would enable it to absorb U.S. security assistance without much difficulty.

Concept Development

Table A.1 outlines a specific, measurable, achievable, relevant/results-oriented, and time-bound plan for attaining the end state of building the Bandarian air force's airlift capacity for peacekeeping operations. It does this by establishing partner-based intermediate objectives or milestones that would logically precede the end state and positing effects that would indicate whether these objectives had been accomplished, as well as the responsibilities for achieving them (columns 1, 2, and 3 from the left). The table also lists several kinds of security cooperation activities that could enable the United States and Bandaria to directly achieve desired effects and, indirectly, the intermediate objectives and end state. The rightmost column indicates the U.S. government offices that would be primarily responsible for overseeing the implementation of the listed security cooperation activities.

The strategic/mission analysis and concept development of the above partial country plan are able to compensate for the inability of

Table A.1
Conceptual Plan for Achieving SMART Objectives

Near-Term Objective (2 years)	Desired Effects	Office of Primary Responsibility	Activities	Offices of Primary Responsibility
BAF has the airlift capability and capacity to support a battalion size regional PKO for three months (illustrative objective 10).	• U.S. and Bandaria jointly develop a program for improving and sustaining BAF's medium airlift capacity to support regional PKOs. • BAF medium air transport fleet achieves an average mission-capable rate of 60 percent. • BAF provides airlift to battalion-size force during PKO or PKO exercise.	CCMD Air Component	Needs/capabilities assessment	Air Component Command
			Air transport exercise observer	Air Force Materiel Command
			Defense cooperation symposium	Commerce Department
			Medium airlift maintenance and training case	Security cooperation office
			Bilateral exercise	CCMD
			External evaluation	OSD

Mid-Term Objective (5 years)	Desired Effects	Office of Primary Responsibility	Activities	Offices of Primary Responsibility
BAF has the airlift capability and capacity to support two separate battalion-size regional PKOs for six months.	• BAF expands the size of its medium airlift fleet by 30 percent. • BAF achieves an average annual mission-capable rate of 75 percent. • BAF provides airlift to battalion-size forces in two separate locations during PKO or PKO exercise.	CCMD Air Component	Senior leader engagement	Air Force Secretariat/HQs
			Medium airlift modernization case	Security cooperation office
			Airlift aircrew exchanges	Air Force Secretariat
			AMC Rodeo participant	Air Force Mobility Command
			Regional exercise	CCMD
			External evaluation	OSD

Table A.1—Continued

Long-Term Objective (7 years)	Desired Effects	Office of Primary Responsibility	Activities	Offices of Primary Responsibility
BAF has the airlift capability and capacity to support a brigade-size regional PKO for one year.	• BAF medium air transport fleet achieves an average annual mission-capable rate of 90 percent. BAF provides airlift to brigade-size force during PKO or PKO exercise.	CCMD Air Component	Airlift aircrew exchanges	Air Force Secretariat
			Medium airlift sustainment case	Security cooperation office
			Regional exercise	CCMD
			External evaluation	OSD

NOTE: BAF = Bandarian air force; PKO = peacekeeping operation.

the Bandaria airlift objective to meet all of the SMART criteria. For example, the strategic/mission analysis demonstrates the objective's relevance/results-orientation by linking it to national- and theater-level strategic priorities and indicating that the partner needs the desired capability. It also builds a case for the objective's achievability by describing the partner's willingness and capacity to work with the United States in achieving the objective, as well as the U.S. government's ability to effectively engage with the partner. For its part, the conceptual plan enhances the specificity and measurability of airlift objectives by spelling out desired effects, such as a specified increase in the mission-capable rate of the airlift fleet, detailing the kinds of security cooperation activities that are needed to achieve these effects, and indicating which offices are primarily responsible for accomplishing objectives and conducting activities.

Abbreviations

AME	assessment, monitoring, and evaluation
CCMD	combatant command
CCP	country cooperation plan
CENTCOM	U.S. Central Command
CSCP	country security cooperation plan
DoD	U.S. Department of Defense
EUCOM	U.S. European Command
EUCOM J7	EUCOM Exercises and Assessments Directorate
G-TSCMIS	Global Theater Security Cooperation Management Information System
IMO	intermediate military objective
LOA	line of activity
LOE	line of effort
MOE	measure of effect
MOEi	measure of effect indicator
MOP	measure of performance
MOPi	measure of performance indicator

OPR	office of primary responsibility
OSD	Office of the Secretary of Defense
PACOM	U.S. Pacific Command
PACOM J4	PACOM Logistics, Engineering, and Security Cooperation Directorate
PACOM J45	PACOM Security Assistance and Cooperative Program Division
PACOM J5	PACOM Strategic Planning and Policy Directorate
PACOM J83	PACOM Strategic Assessments Division
SAS Plan	database interface developed by EUCOM's J5 Research and Analysis Office (SAS stands for a term that is no longer used)
SCO	security cooperation organization
SDO	senior defense official
SMART	specific, measurable, achievable, relevant and results-oriented, and time-bound
SOUTHCOM	U.S. Southern Command
SOUTHCOM J54	SOUTHCOM Security Cooperation Division
SOUTHCOM J55	SOUTHCOM Strategic Planning Division
SOUTHCOM J85	SOUTHCOM Acquisition Support Division
TCP	Theater Campaign Plan

References

Boyd, John, Science, Strategy and War: The Strategic Theory of John Boyd, New York: Routledge, 2007.

Defense Institute of Security Assistance Management, *The Management of Security Cooperation* ("Green Book"), August 2015. As of October 9, 2015: http://www.disam.dsca.mil/_pages/resources/default.aspx?section=publications&type=greenbook

Doran, George T., "There's a S.M.A.R.T. Way to Write Management's Goals and Objectives," *Management Review*, Vol. 70, No. 11, 1981, pp. 35–36.

Drucker, Peter F., *The Practice of Management*, New York: Harper & Row, 1954.

———, *The Essential Drucker: Selections from the Management Works of Peter F. Drucker*, 1st ed., New York: HarperBusiness, 2001.

Guffey, Rich, and Jim Welton, "Strategy-to-Task Implementation Through Country Cooperation Plans and Lines of Activity," EUCOM briefing document, May 13, 2015.

Joint Publication 5-0, *Joint Operational Planning*, Washington, D.C.: Joint Chiefs of Staff, August 11, 2011.

Kloecker, Robert L., "Implementing the Commander's Strategy: Theater Campaign Framework," EUCOM briefing document, April 29, 2014.

Latham, Gary P., and Gary A. Yukl, "A Review of Research on the Application of Goal Setting in Organizations," *Academy of Management Journal*, Vol. 18, No. 4, 1975, pp. 824–845.

Locke, Edwin A., Karyll N. Shaw, Lise M. Saari, and Gary P. Latham, "Goal Setting and Task Performance: 1969–1980," *Psychological Bulletin*, Vol. 90, No. 1, 1981, pp. 125–152.

Moroney, Jennifer D. P., David E. Thaler, and Joe Hogler, *Review of Security Cooperation Mechanisms Combatant Commands Utilize to Build Partner Capacity*, Santa Monica, Calif.: RAND Corporation, RR-413-OSD, 2013. As of November 20, 2015: http://www.rand.org/pubs/research_reports/RR413.html

Perry, Walter L., Stuart E. Johnson, Stephanie Pezard, Gillian S. Oak, David Stebbins, and Chaoling Feng, *Defense Institution Building: An Assessment*, Santa Monica, Calif.: RAND Corporation, RR-1176-OSD, 2016.

Schunk, Dale H., and Barry Zimmerman, *Handbook of Self-Regulation of Learning and Performance*, Abingdon, UK: Routledge, 2011.

U.S. Department of Defense Security Cooperation Reform Task Force, *Phase I Report*, Washington, D.C., 2011.

U.S. European Command, website, no date. As of February 26, 2016: http://www.eucom.mil/

———, ECJ5 Research and Analysis Division, untitled SAS Plan instructional document, April 29, 2015.

U.S. Pacific Command, website, no date. As of February 26, 2016: http://www.pacom.mil/

U.S. Southern Command, website, no date. As of February 26, 2016: http://www.southcom.mil/

Wade, D. T., "Goal Setting in Rehabilitation: An Overview of What, Why and How," *Clinical Rehabilitation*, Vol. 23, No. 4, April 1, 2009, pp. 291–295.

The White House, "Fact Sheet: U. S. Security Sector Assistance Policy," Presidential Policy Directive 23, April 5, 2013. As of October 16, 2015: https://www.whitehouse.gov/the-press-office/2013/04/05/fact-sheet-us-security-sector-assistance-policy

———, *The National Security Strategy of the United States of America*, Washington, D.C., February 2015. As of November 16, 2015: https://www.whitehouse.gov/sites/default/files/docs/2015_national_security_strategy.pdf